BE THE CHANGE:
BE THE DIFFERENCE

BE THE CHANGE

BE THE DIFFERENCE

How can I be the change
that makes a difference
in the world? **A series of
inspirational answers.**

IN AID OF THE
HOPE FOUNDATION

978-0-9931143-3-5

Prepared for publication by
DROMBEG BOOKS
Leap, Skibbereen, County Cork

Tel: 028 33991 / 087 2720028
drombegbooks@gmail.com

CONTENTS

MAUREEN FORREST
Introduction   1

JULIE ALDRIDGE
Art therapy tutor   9

BIBI BASKIN
TV presenter   13

EILEEN BENNETT
Founder and CEO of Horses Connect   17

SEAN BARRETT
Politician   23

DANIEL BRENNAN
Author and life coach   27

PETER CORNISH
Author and founder of Dzogchen Beara meditation centre   33

PAT THE BARBER CROWLEY
Author and speaker on self-inquiry   39

CLARE DOWLING
Novelist and screenwriter   43

MYLES DUNGAN
Broadcaster and author   47

JOHN EVOY
Founder of the Irish Men's Sheds Association (IMSA)   49

MEIMEI FOX
Author, editor, and life coach   55

VANESSA FOX O'LOUGHLIN
Publishing consultant and literary scout   59

TEENA GATES
Author, broadcaster, and motivational speaker   63

MARK PATRICK HEDERMAN
Benedictine monk and writer 65

TOM HICKEY
Journalist and blogger 69

CON HURLEY
Journalist, life coach and author 73

RICHARD KEARNEY
Philosopher and author 79

KATE KERRIGAN
Novelist and newspaper columnist 83

CHUCK KRUGER
Author and poet 87

MARY MALONE
Novelist 91

DAVID McCARTHY
Human rights and mental health activist 95

HUGH McFADDEN
Poet and journalist 101

MATTIE McGRATH
Politician 109

PETER McVERRY
Priest and campaigner 113

ROISIN MEANEY
Novelist 117

MICHAEL MURPHY
Farmer and businessman 121

ELLIE O'BYRNE
Journalist 125

GRETT O'CONNOR
Television and radio journalist 133

FINBAR O'MAHONY
Management consultant 137

MATT PADWICK
Author 145

ALAN POWER
Head gardener and radio personality 151

SUZANNE POWER
Author, broadcaster and columnist 155

FRANCISCO REBOLLO
Author and airline pilot 159

GILLIAN RIORDAN
Psychotherapist 163

DAVID ROSS
Farmer and pastor 169

PETER THOMPSON
Journalist 175

JOHN WATERS
Author and journalist 183

DEDICATION

Dedicated to the memory of Aunty Joan,

who always taught us, by example, to think of others.

FOREWORD

IT WAS after hearing Maureen Forrest speaking about her personal philosophy to a group of us in Waterford that I decided to put this book together. The result I hope will provide encouragement and inspiration to anyone who is pondering how they can make a contribution to the world, big or small, that will make a difference.

The writers are a mixture of the well-known and not so well-known, but whatever their background they have in each case something of great interest to say that is born out of their own individual experiences. And one theme dominates throughout, that where positivity exists, all is possible.

I would like to thank Maureen Forrest and the HOPE team for inspiring me, the wonderful members of the WCC business group, those who became contributors despite busy schedules, those who made contributions in lieu of written submissions.

Catherine O'Byrne Casey

How can I be the change that will make a difference in the world?

By MAUREEN FORREST,
Founder and Honorary Director of The Hope Foundation

"What counts in life is not the mere fact that we have lived. It is what difference we have made to the lives of others that will determine the significance of the life we lead." – Nelson Mandela

IT WAS a school visit from a Sister of the Medical Missionaries of Mary that planted the ideas and visions that would drive me towards making a difference to those who needed it the most.

This was my start, my catalyst, my moment of inspiration but it has been my experiences over the following decades that keep

1

my motivation alive. Coming from a large family of twelve children, caring and sharing started the day that I was born. Although I must admit I did not jump straight into life in the development sector. I spent my early years working in Cork, London and Shannon Airport. Then I met my future husband Dick and moved back home as a farmer's wife to East Cork. However, my desire to remain aware of the issues in global development never decreased and led me to study Development Studies in University College Cork.

During the Ethiopian famine in the early 1980s, I began fundraising for Goal, an organisation with which my sister Ber was volunteering in Ethiopia. In the late 1980s, Dick and I were lucky enough to have been in a position to holiday in South Africa and Swaziland visiting friends. While we were there, we visited refugee centres run by GOAL on the borders of Mozambique and Swaziland, where we witnessed firsthand the appalling horrors the Mozambican civil war visited upon that country's citizens. After that visit I knew that I had to make a life-long commitment to helping the world's poor.

My first overseas volunteer assignment was with GOAL in war-torn Somalia in the early 1990s, where I worked in a feeding centre with 2,000 children. Gunfire, shootings, starvation and death were part of my daily life. Living in a war zone is a frightening place to be. One incident which juxtaposed my life in Ireland with that of my humanitarian work was when our camp was shot at and I remember lying on the floor thinking, '*I don't want to die on my own in a foreign country*'.

But there were always more people to be helped. Thousands were still dying of starvation on a daily basis. Still, I reminded myself that '*you can only do what you can do*'. I still believe that. If I managed to save or change only one life, my efforts would have been worthwhile. Two years after my time in Somalia, I went to work in a refugee camp in Goma in the Congo, just over the border from Rwanda – 350,000 refugees were seeking sanctuary in the camp, fleeing Rwanda and the worst genocide since World War II. The mass graves will always remain etched in my mind. As will the image of a bulldozer just dumping the bodies of men, women and children into a pit – on top of the decomposing bodies which were already buried there.

It was a visit to Kolkata – formerly known as Calcutta – in India in 1993 that proved to be the life-changing experience that set me on the path to where I am today. On that trip I met the late Mother Teresa. She had a huge impact on me personally and on the direction that my life would take. There was nothing that could prepare me for the horror that was Kolkata. The streets were home to thousands of people. Whole families lived on the pavements. The street was their kitchen, their bedroom, their sitting-room, their bathroom – they lived their entire lives in public view. I remember seeing the treatment of the poor and thinking how could people pass them as if they did not exist? Even now these initial thoughts are never far from my mind. I spent my time visiting the slums and the streets of Kolkata. It was at this time that I met with Geeta who would later be instrumental in helping me in establish the Indian office of HOPE.

'They had no freedom. They had no choice. They had no hope.'

It was on my return visit to Kolkata, accompanied by my daughter Louise, in 1999, that I decided to spearhead the establishment of a new organisation, The Hope Foundation. There was something about Kolkata – and the fate of the thousands of street children – that grabbed my heartstrings and would not let go. Nearly a quarter of a million street children in Kolkata try to survive against all odds in putrid squalor, sifting through mountains of refuse in the rubbish dumps in order to eke out a living for themselves and their families. These children exist in abject poverty. To see this, relentlessly, every day of my six weeks there was utterly heartbreaking. More heartbreaking was the knowledge that, though I was free to leave, these children, like their parents before them, had no such choice. They had no freedom. They had no choice. They had no hope.

Instinctively, I knew that I could help make a real, positive difference by concentrating my efforts on this one city and her hundreds of thousands of street children. To me, the streets felt like the refugee camps of Africa, where the poor, desolate and forgotten members of society were left to rot. I knew that I could give these children the hope they needed – the hope they deserved. The first thing homeless children need is a home and so when I got back to Cork I set about raising funds for the first HOPE home. Getting the Foundation up and running took a lot of planning and I was fortunate to have fantastic friends and family around me to help me in my cause. I don't think I could have foreseen then what HOPE would grow into. The phenomenal growth has presented myself and my team with lots of challenges along the way but has enabled us to now offer more opportunities to the children of Kolkata. This remains my motivation and driving force. I am deeply committed to getting as many children into education as possible. Each child deserves to be given a better opportunity in life, carve out a sustainable livelihood for themselves and break out of the cycle of poverty.

None of the great work of the Hope Foundation could have been achieved without the hard-working and dedicated team of HOPE staff and volunteers in Ireland, India, the UK and Germany along with the support of our local Indian partners. Their commitment along with the phenomenal generosity of the people of Ireland have enabled HOPE to develop into the charity it is today. Since its establishment, HOPE's battle against child labour and child trafficking has highlighted the unbearable suffering endured by the children of Kolkata. The organisation has successfully rescued thousands of children from a life of misery. Thanks to the support of the public and the Irish Government, HOPE now funds and operates more than sixty projects

in Kolkata, working with street and slum children, their families
and communities. Projects covers areas such as shelter, healthcare,
education, vocational training, child protection and anti-traffick-
ing, anti-child labour and child rights advocacy. The projects include eight child-protection homes, a children's hospital, an HIV/
AIDS hospice and a drug-rehabilitation centre for children and
teenagers. Other services, such as HOPE's primary healthcare
programme's mobile clinics and Night Watch emergency-rescue
project, extend across vast areas of the city and reach out to thousands who have no access to state services.

Education

It is through these services that we are making our greatest impact and making a difference to the lives of some of the world's
most needy. We have come a long way from our initial projects
and that is duly reflected in the impact that we can show for our
work. Across our three main programme areas we are seeing year-
on-year improvements in results and in those we are reaching out
to. In the last year alone we have managed to engage with, support and help 2,268 children through our Holistic Education programme. This has seen them provided with educational support
in addition to nutritional, psychological, health and recreational
support for their development. Our work in education has also
seen many thousands of children gain access to schools to continue their formal education. Earlier this year I was delighted to read
that one of the girls from our PBKOJP Girls' Protection Home
has recently enrolled in college to study for her bachelor degree
in geography, the first girl from that home to do so.

Healthcare

Healthcare has obviously been one of our main areas of concern
and one where we constantly strive to provide as much help for

the people of Kolkata as we can manage. Anyone who has been to Kolkata can attest to the situation whereby when you mix a lack of sanitation, a lack of potable water, the extreme living conditions with overwhelming poverty and limited access to healthcare services then you are fighting against a healthcare disaster. As a result of this suffering, disease and death had become the norm for many thousands of people living in the slums. Our work has sought to fight back against this problem and we have made great advances in this regard. The opening of our HOPE Hospital was a major step in the fight against inadequate healthcare in Kolkata. Between 2013 and 2014 we treated 10,336 patients through our in-patient and out-patient departments. This is a remarkable achievement and earlier this year our commitment to healthcare has been further strengthened by the opening of our own pharmacy in the hospital. The hospital is not a lone venture in our work in healthcare, we are also fortunate to have very dedicated and professional staff who run our ambulance service, our mental illness clinics, our personal hygiene and awareness clinics amongst other projects. The problem of healthcare is one that will not be easily eradicated from the lives of the slum dwelling people of Kolkata but it is one that, I am delighted to say, we are working hard to alleviate.

Child Protection

Along with our great work in healthcare and education, our protection projects were last year able to reach out and help a large number of children who otherwise would have been left to wander the streets and rubbish dumps of Kolkata. Providing protection for the children of Kolkata has been a key motivation since setting up The Hope Foundation and that drive and determination has not waned since those first days. Child labour is awful, and India unfortunately has suffered terribly with this blight. Streets, shops, houses and rubbish piles are still filled with children who have been forced to work to scrape together a measly exist-ence. Thousands more children are regularly trafficked into a life of hell as child-prostitutes. Our child protection projects aim to guard children from physical, emotional and sexual abuse as well as neglect. Through our Protection Homes, Emergency Response Unit and Crisis Intervention Centres 1,116 children have direct-ly benefitted in the last year. When I am in Kolkata I like to stay in the Panditya home, one of the HOPE protection homes for girls. I love spending time with the children and I adore watch-ing them grow up to be well-adjusted adults – though I must admit that sharing a bathroom with twenty girls every morn-ing can be quite a challenge! It is in these moments that I can see how we are making a difference. My journey with HOPE is, and has always been, hugely rewarding. Through HOPE so many lives have been saved. Thousands of children have been educated and will have a secure future. The greatest heartbreak but also the greatest joy during my lifetime has been and remains my work with the poorest of the poor among the street children of Kol-kata – I know that I can never abandon them. As long as there are 250,000 street children in Kolkata, The HOPE Foundation will have 250,000 reasons to exist.

I want to sincerely thank each and every one of you for your support, it could not have happened without you. I would also like to extend a special thanks to Catherine O'Bryne Casey with-out whom this book would not have been possible.

HOPE is ours; we share its journey, its joys, its sorrows and we stand together to witness the changes in our society. The book that you are holding in your hands is a reflection of huge gener-osity: the generosity of those who have cared enough to buy it and the generosity of those who contributed to it. Talented peo-ple from all walks of life generously and selflessly gave of their time and talents to each write a piece for this book. They did so because they, too, were touched by the plight of the babies who are born on the pavements and in the slums of Kolkata. They did so because they wanted to contribute to housing, feeding, educating, protecting and helping thousands of innocent children in Kolkata. Each piece in this book holds 'Hope' as its central theme and is a wonderful testament to the power of hope. It is hope, after all, that keeps us all going and pushes us into 'making a difference'.

JULIE ALDRIDGE
Art therapy tutor

I WOULD like to assert from the outset my belief that every human being that arrives here on Earth makes a difference to the world, whether consciously or unconsciously. As a species, despite all our cultural, scientific, and technological efforts, we seem only to be on the nursery slopes of understanding our selves and our motivations as individuals.

In this time-limited life experience, the inevitability of change seems to be a given, and yet psychologically as humans we often defend ourselves or resist this fact. As a species it appears we have overreached ourselves in relation to the impact we have had on the wider context of human existence and all the other creatures and manifold forms of life with

Julie Aldridge and her partner have lived in Ireland for over twenty years. Julie works as a part-time art therapy tutor and continues to paint and write poetry. They live with an independently minded sheepdog in a far flung part of rural Ireland.

which we are privileged to coexist.

In 1993, aged 28, I cut myself free from the familiarity of a secure job and home, city life, good friends and my remaining family – a father and a younger sister – in order to move to Ireland with my life partner of ten years at the time. I experienced this as a kind of self-imposed exile of inner necessity. If my comfortable existence needed a challenge then arriving jobless, homeless, unmarried and unknown in a far-flung part of Ireland, then this was it.

In this time-limited life experience, the inevitability of change seems to be a given, and yet…we often resist this fact.

For the first six months we were itinerant and as we met many different people we made a kind of Pilgrim's Progress through the many challenges, pitfalls and opportunities which commonly beset the stranger in a strange land. We lost money, some of our idealism and many of our assumptions, but we also met with kindness, curiosity and Irish warmth. This was a journey in search of the 'unthought known' and we never entirely lost hope or the sense of it being an act of faith.

Twenty years or more on, things appear rather more settled and I feel I have found my niche in life. At this stage, I can also acknowledge the many ways in which I am ill equipped for this rural life. For instance, I failed to master the art of driving, despite public transport being more than tenuous in these parts. Neither of us are very practical but we do possess great powers of endurance and stoicism. We lived for over three years without any water supply. Every visitor who came to us was encouraged to bring or take away containers with, or for, drinking water. The place looked more like a water processing plant than I imagine is the case at the Ballygowan factory. Throughout this trial by no water, I was made to search every avenue for a solution to this perplexing problem in a country renowned for its rainfall . Ultimately an answer came from a deep and powerful experience of connection to the natural environment here, coupled with cooperation within the local farming community, who had also suffered the lack of suitable water for themselves and their animals.

At this time of year, I set a small kitchen garden but I now know I will never be a farmer, I will never be Irish, I will not have children (though I have been the potential guardian of two small people). If self-knowledge is the measure of success, then believe I am learning so much more about love and the art of living than if I had chosen to stay with the safe and familiar lifestyle I had previously created.

BIBI BASKIN

TV presenter

IN 2001 I went to India on a first visit. It was meant to be a holiday during the course of which I would further my life-long pursuit of the Indian system of mind/body health, Ayurveda. I had planned to stay three weeks. But that country, its delights, its problems and in particular its wonderful people somehow took hold of me and I stayed for fifteen years. Yes, FIFTEEN!

I went as a typical middle-class western woman and I came back humbled and tempered by the Indian way of life. The striving, the hopes, the sacrifices all chastised me and I realised that India had changed me for the better.

The first shift happened before I even

Bibi Baskin is a former presenter on RTE, and was the first woman in Ireland to have a TV chat-show of her own. She has also worked on both radio and TV in the UK. She then moved to India where she bought a dilapidated landmark building in Kerala, south India, which she converted into a Heritage Hotel and in which she spent fifteen very happy years.

reached the hotel in Trivandrum, south India, my first destination. A big white Ambassador taxi had picked me up at the airport and as we bumped along a fairly pot-holed road, I thought, 'There's an awful lot of people around.' An understatement of India's huge population! It was something I would have to get used to.

Sometimes in life it's not enough to learn the life lessons. It's even better when we get them reinforced later on.

And then I saw her. An Indian lady, possibly in her 40s, sitting on the roadside with only a coconut palm for shelter from the raging sun. Her job was to smash stones with a small, rusty tool. Naturally I thought it was a lousy job. I had no idea then that Indian women do construction work. But what caught my eye more than anything was the glorious shocking pink sari she wore to that job. I looked down at my white t-shirt and beige trousers and I saw at a glance how I paled in significance. That was my first introduction to the rainbow of colours and the vibrancy that is a normal part of everyday Indian life. I don't wear white and beige much anymore.

As I settled into my new existence I found that my experience of living and learning from India involved three different stages. Firstly there was the rosy-tinted specs phase when I was a greenhorn tourist. Then everything, everybody and most systems were all perfect. I would ask myself the uninformed questions that a lot of first-time tourists do – like how come everyone is so poor yet everyone is smiling. And more banalities like that.

It changed somewhat when I rented a house. I was still without a job but having to do the normal chores of running a simple home. Like going to pay the electricity bill where I discovered that there was no sign of modest western queuing. It was rather more like a free-for-all. I didn't much like it. No discipline, no order. Then discovering there were official power cuts each day and wondering where to put my sweaty brow when there was no air-conditioning no fan and no light. I needed less inconvenience. It didn't happen and I had to adjust.

It was during this adjustment period that I started to realise that in a highly bureaucratic country like India where at best the wheels move slowly it doesn't pay to be impatient. Not only that, but at local level Indians don't like impatience and they won't re-act very well to you if you go off on a rant. I was being further chastised.

The third learning phase began when I started to work. Having sold my home in Europe, I bought an old, dilapidated land-mark building, refurbished it and eventually turned it into a Her-itage Hotel, recognized by the Central Government of India. This project went from having forty local men working on the refur-bishment, finding an Indian business partner, which is a legal re-quirement, and turning this empty building into a fully-equipped and fully-staffed four-star hotel. It worked. We were written up in *The Sunday Times*, London, as 'one of the ten best sleeps in India'. But this could never have happened unless co-operative Indian colleagues met me more than half-way as I got to know the In-dian way of doing things. Now I was in the thick of India and for me it proved to be a great meeting of east and west.

But sometimes in life it's not enough to learn the life lessons. It's even better when we get them reinforced later on.

And so after fifteen years I decided that it was time to come home. There's something about home, isn't there? And I felt that the time was right. But inevitably I came back to a different Ire-land. Of course there were many semblances of familiarity but the Celtic Tiger, the burgeoning of the economy, had happened in the meantime followed by the inevitable slump. And people had changed.

The significant and worrying change that I witnessed was that those who were lucky enough to have jobs – and there were too many who didn't – they were working themselves so hard that I immediately questioned their quality of life. Gym in the morning, commute to work, long hours in the office, miserable sandwich from a petrol station for lunch *al desko*, an event in the evening for networking purposes to grow the business, home again, a microwaved meal with little nutrition and then to bed with the laptop to catch up on Social Media. Phew!

Where was the fun, I asked myself? Life is supposed to have fun. And anyway why would people want to work themselves almost to death? And for what exactly?

It still continues. But I am not part of that pack. India, for all its own extremes, had taught me a Middle Way. The thing that's also called Life/Work balance. The western world is not very good at it. But whereas there may not be any conscious awareness of this principle in India, it is silently at work. Indians still put family and friends first. And in order to do that you need to give family/friends your time, your attention, your affection. Back in Ireland I found people who almost needed an appointment to see their nearest and dearest.

They have no time, they tell me. No time even for themselves and their own relaxation. But there could be if they made a conscious choice to create it.

One day certainly there will be no time because they or you will have moved into the eternity plane. Maybe that means that there will be endless time. But if it exists, it won't be like the time we have now as mind/body beings,

So I would say slow down. Ask yourself what's it all for. Take a day off here and there and don't feel guilty. And spend time with people you love. Because one day it will most definitely be too late.

I had to go to India to learn this. India, I thank you. Namaste.

'Live as if you were to die tomorrow. Learn as if you were to live forever.' - Mahatma Gandhi

EILEEN BENNETT
Founder and CEO of Horses Connect

WHEN I was growing up, change was something to be avoided at all costs. My parents' generation took comfort in knowing that everything would unfold in a certain, predictable way. There was a protocol for behaving at every stage of life. There were clear rules laid down by Church and State to be obeyed. Every rule was based in fear and carried dire warnings of what could befall anyone who dared to break them. You knew who you were supposed to be in those days. Apart from unavoidable catastrophes, change came slowly.

My life was quite different. I learned from a young age to roll with the punches and to deal with the unexpected. I eventually learned

Eileen Bennett is CEO and co-founder of Horses Connect, a social enterprise based in Galway delivering equine-based programs to people of all ages who are experiencing a range of challenges. Horses Connect is the realisation of a lifelong dream for Eileen and perfectly satisfies four equal passions: teaching, learning, people and horses.

that change, though often uncomfortable and scary, is always good.

Change is one of life's few constants and yet change itself is always changing. In the past ten years, the pace of change has dramatically increased. Today's most innovative piece of technology will be obsolete next week. More importantly, our attitude to change has also shifted. More and more of us are recognising and accepting that change ultimately leads to improvement. To expect everything to stay the same is a guaranteed recipe for stress and unhappiness. Could the human race be growing up?

The change I would like to see in the world involves a renewed humility and a reconnection with beauty and truth.

The evolution of our attitude to change can be compared to our personal emotional development. We move from being needy and demanding to being rebellious teenagers and eventually reach adulthood. The world is full of people at every stage of this cycle but society at large seems to starting to behave in a grown up way – some of the time.

Perhaps the biggest and most positive change I'm aware of is that we are finally beginning to see ourselves and each other as we really are. The human race is slowly waking up to its own true nature. We are starting to appreciate what really matters.

In my teens the words of the poet John Keats – 'Beauty is truth, truth beauty. That is all ye know on earth and all ye need to know' – resonated and have stayed with me ever since. All we need to know is that truth and beauty are the same thing. If we seek truth, we will always find beauty. Everywhere and in everyone.

To try to understand Life, the Universe and Everything in all its amazing complexity is like trying to appreciate a breath-taking view through a keyhole. Some have bigger, or better positioned, vantage points than others, but every one of us is limited in our capacity to comprehend the vastness of the universe and the meaning of life. Traditionally, we have used religion to explain it all, but science is teaching us that 'God did it' is not a satisfactory answer.

When you look to nature and animals, you get a much clearer understanding of what it's all about. There is no pretence outside the human race. We act like we know it all, when in truth the further we have moved away from nature, the closer we get to ignorance.

The change I would like to see in the world involves a renewed humility and a reconnection with beauty and truth. There is so much to learn from the innocents: nature, our fellow creatures, children and, most importantly, anybody who does not conform to society's definition of 'normal'.

I first became aware of the human-animal connection when a cross-bred dog called Caesar came into my world. I was a shy and messed-up pre-teen and he became my best friend, confidante, counsellor and saviour. He carried me into young adulthood and sent me on my way, knowing that I was worth loving.

In 1976 I was working in Manchester in a hostel for teenage girls, labelled 'emotionally disturbed' by the health system. One of my jobs was to bring them on outings, so I took them to the stables in Heaton Park. A few of the girls would come riding with me but some of them had no interest in horses. They only came along to hang out with the boys. It very quickly became obvious to them that the only way to hang out with boys working in a busy stable yard was to literally 'muck in' with the jobs they were doing, so these girls would groom and sweep and shovel. Staff in the hostel always remarked how 'different' those girls were for a few days after being with horses. They were calmer, happier somehow, and much more open to engaging in conversation.

The idea for setting up a human-animal healing centre was conceived that year, but it has been a very long gestation. Research into what was being done in other parts of the world became much easier when the internet was invented. By then, animal-facilitated interactions were well-established in America, Australia and England. I was especially drawn to horses, because while their size can be an added challenge for some people, their gentleness and kindness acts as a catalyst and a valuable teaching tool.

It has taken almost forty years to get to the point of realising the dream of allowing animals in general and horses in particular to show us the way to be who we really are. Who we really are is hidden under generations of conditioning and layers of accepted beliefs. We may have gadgets that allow us to speak to each other anywhere in the world in real time, but we have lost touch with our souls. We have forgotten that we are star stuff. We have come to believe in the labels and the limitations. We have lost our connection to our own truth and beauty.

With animals, there are no facades. All communication is pure and honest. There is nothing to hide. Labels simply do not exist. Life is black and white and simple.

When you put a person who is 'damaged' in some way in contact with a horse, magic happens. The less the individual is able to connect with the world through 'normal' channels, the quicker the bond with the horse happens. The more willing the person is to shed all traces of pretence and to acknowledge and accept their own true beauty, the deeper and more powerful the connection with the horse.

It's not easy to accept our own beauty and truth. Marianne Williamson said it perfectly: 'Our deepest fear is not that we are inadequate. Our deepest fear is that we are powerful beyond measure. It is our light, not our darkness that most frightens us. We ask ourselves, Who am I to be brilliant, gorgeous, talented, and fabulous? Actually, who are you not to be?'

Finding proof of our shortcomings is much simpler. We can all recite examples of how we don't measure up and where we fail as good human beings. But when we can begin to see the light in ourselves and others, everything changes.

Depending on your belief system, the story of Adam and Eve in the Garden of Eden is a true account of how the human race began or a work of fiction. Either way, it provides a really useful analogy for the evolution of our psyche. In the beginning, all was truth and beauty. Then we learned about deceit and shame and distrust and became obsessed with self-protection. We focused on what was wrong with ourselves, each other and the world around us and lost sight of everything that was right and beautiful. This shift in attitude from the open and trusting to the guarded and suspicious was nurtured by religion. Nobody was safe. Even newborn babies were tainted by 'original sin' and started life having to apologise and make amends.

When you stand in the company of an animal, or you sit under a tree, you know that you are being fully accepted for who you are.

We are complex creatures, very fond of over-thinking and analysing other people's motives. When you stand in the company of an animal, or you sit under a tree, you know that you are being fully accepted for who you are, in that moment. Nothing else matters; not the colour of your skin, your belief system, what you're wearing, your bank balance, your life experiences or your plans for tomorrow.

In reality, there is no 'magic' in animal assisted interactions. The horse or dog or cat doesn't have any 'special power's to allow it to see into our souls. It is just doing the only thing it knows how to do. It is simply being a horse or dog or cat. The difficult part for us is that the animal is asking us to also simply be, and that can be quite a challenge. Some of us have forgotten who we are. Some of us don't like who we are and some of us are ashamed of who we are. Some of us carry so much pain and fear inside us that we have built strong defences to protect ourselves.

But, no matter what our personal history has loaded onto us, beneath it all is the innate truth and beauty that is our true nature. That is what the animal sees and reacts to. The animal sees it because it is always there. It could be very deeply buried and well disguised, but truth and beauty can never be hidden from anyone who wants to see it.

I don't like the word 'god'. It has too many associations with oppression and fear. I prefer to use the word 'Good' when referring to the source of all beauty and truth. I hope Marianne Williamson will forgive me for editing her words:

'We are all meant to shine, as children do. We were born to make manifest the glory of Good that is within us. It is not just in some of us; it is in everyone and as we let our own light shine, we unconsciously give others permission to do the same. As we are liberated from our own fear, our presence automatically liberates others.'

So, while the change I would like to see in the world is a renewed acceptance and recognition of the truth and beauty all around us and within us, the most challenging part is acknowledging my own worth. It is much easier to look out and find the good in other people, animals and situations but for real and lasting change to happen, my gaze needs to turn inwards first. And we all need to do the same.

Shine on!

SEAN BARRETT

Politician

THE GREAT Scottish author John Buchan has claimed that the practice of politics is both an honourable and noble profession. Politicians have the capacity to enhance their community, their country and even the world in their endeavours to draft policies that are designed to shape society and enrich the lives of their fellow human beings.

In his ill-fated 1968 US Presidential campaign the late US Senator Robert F Kennedy enunciated what was, in my opinion, the perfect political manifesto when he stated in *To Seek a Newer World*, 'Each time someone stands up for an ideal, or endeavours to improve the lot of others, or seeks to correct an injustice, he sends forth a tiny ripple of hope. And then,

Sean Barrett was first elected to the Dáil for Dun Laoghaire in 1981 as a member of Fine Gael and served as Minister for Sport from 1982 to 1987 and Minister for Defence and the Marine from 1994 to 1997. He was Ceann Comhairle of the Dáil from 2011 to 2016.

the ripples, gaining in strength from a million different centres of energy and daring, grow into a tide that can sweep aside the mightiest walls of oppression and indifference.'

In advancing the needs of people who require housing accommodation, educational or health services from the local authority, politicians can be the engines of both progress and justice. Politics helps us to make government work, and in the words of Tom Kettle, Irish writer, barrister and politician, who died at the Battle of the Somme, 'Politics is the State in action – the great human conspiracy against hunger and cold, against loneliness and ignorance and which redeems from despair that great adventure that we call human life – In short, the promotion of the common good for all our citizens.' (*The Day's Burden*)

The early 21ˢᵗ Century has produced a number of global challenges that, if adequately addressed, would surely transform the lives of the world's population:

- Universal sustainable development in an era of global climate change
- The provision of sufficient clean water for all
- Meeting growing energy demands as cheap fossil fuels diminish
- Reducing the gap between rich and poor ethically
- Balancing population growth with resources
- Transforming authoritarian regimes into democratic systems
- Convergence of communications and information technologies
- Addressing ethnic conflicts, terrorism and Weapons of Mass Destruction
- Changed status of women enhancing the human condition
- Prevention of organised crime networks from becoming global
- Meeting growing energy demands safely and efficiently
- Accelerating scientific and technological breakthroughs for

humanity
- Resolving global decisions using ethical considerations

In today's society, levels of wealth, consumption and ease of living are at a stage virtually unheard of hitherto in human history, resulting in the exponential increase in the use of fossil fuels without regard for the finite amount of these fuels that remain on the planet.

The transformation of our world to one that is just and sustainable was the main objective of Ireland's first-ever Climate Change and Energy Security Bill, which was produced by the Joint Oireachtas Committee on Climate Change and Energy Security, of which I was honoured to be chairman between 2007 and 2011.

It would be my great personal privilege to be instrumental in helping people to create a just and compassionate society.

It would also be my great personal privilege to be instrumental in helping people to create a just and compassionate economic system and society, by addressing the growing disparities of wealth and attaining as many of the aforementioned global goals as possible for the greater good of humanity.

DANIEL BRENNAN

Author and life coach

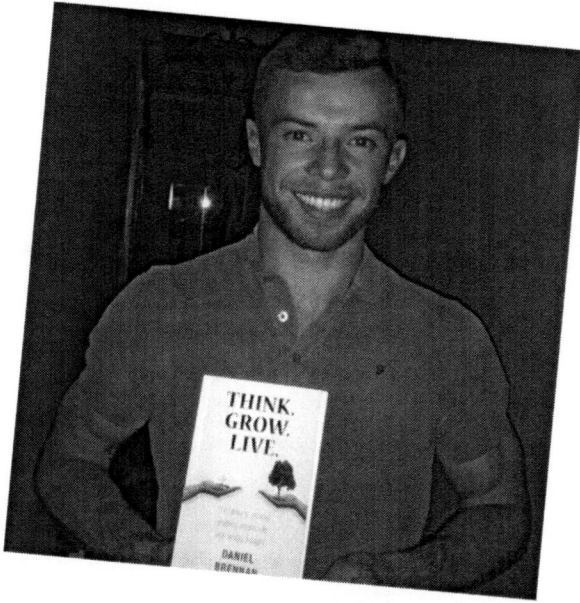

LEARNING TO be a person who lives *from the inside out* is one of the most valuable things I have learned. Circumstances determine most people's feelings and attitude towards the world and towards other people. I believe, however, that you can let your attitude and feelings determine your circumstances. If you can change a few things, you can alter your perception of situations that you might once have thought to be negative.

Most people in the world are very much *out to in* people. Their circumstances affect their feelings and happiness. Being an *out to in* person is not good, because it means you have no control over the only thing in the world that you should and can control – your

In his quest to become a better golfer, Daniel Brennan became interested in learning as much as he could about personal development. His book, *Think. Grow. Live,* charts his exploration of that topic. He runs *uyplifestyle.com,* a web site that helps people 'unlock their true potential'.

thoughts. Obviously we are not robots, so we can't feel great all day every day. But what we can do is try our best to be aware of our thoughts and of how things that we think are negative can actually be positive.

Being an *in to out* person just means that you are aware of situations and circumstances but you control how you react and perceive them, usually choosing to react in a positive manner. Being *in to out* is the best and easiest way to be happy. You may say, 'But what if something happens to me and puts my life at risk, how can I be happy when I know I might die?' The answer is that you can still be happy. Obviously it is going to take more energy to be happy than if you had nothing wrong, but you can certainly choose to be happy. You can sit back and let whatever has happened take over your life or you can say, 'No, I'm not going to let this determine how I feel, I'm going to have a blast until I beat this circumstance.' See what you've done there? You have taken a devastating and clearly bad situation and turned it into something more positive. You are controlling all that you can control and you are channelling your energy in the right direction to enjoy yourself.

Channelling your energy into better thoughts will help you see the world from a much better perspective.

Channelling your energy into better thoughts will help you see the world from a much better perspective. I know many people, some of whom are friends, who always have something negative to say about everyone and everything; I too am guilty of this at times. And we all know how draining negativity like that can be. If, however, you can focus on the positives in the world and the positives in other people then you will bring out the positives in you. Yet again this is all down to self-talk.

When someone does something different, 'out of the ordinary', people will sit up and take notice. But what is the ordinary? The ordinary is monotonous, boring and not a fulfilling life. Doing something different and great is fun and enjoyable and will make you energetic. What you do and how you do it is up to you. Create your own happiness, real happiness, from the inside out.

Out to in...

Out to in people tend to be very up and down in their emotions and feelings. Their circumstances rule their minds and their happiness. Its raining outside, so it's a bad day. No its not a bad day, it's a great day. You are alive, you woke up. You should feel blessed. What makes rain bad is that people tell you it is bad and you believe that it is bad. It can have bad effects on the world, but ultimately that's to do with nature and isn't anything you can control, so why should you worry about it?

Negativity attracts negativity, so the more negative you are, the more negative you and your surroundings will become. I hate my job. Why? You chose to hate your job. What about the millions of people that are homeless and can't get a job? If you hate your job, quit and do something you like. Looking at the world with a more open and in-tune mind will make your days much better. Take a leaf from this chapter and decide to work on being an in to out person. This means that you choose how to feel, how to act and how to think. It will change your life from the minute you start doing it.

A little note on risk-taking. If you want to do something great with your life, you need to take risks and not be afraid to fail. If you hate your job, why would you stay there? You have to? Some circumstances will mean you do have to stay in your job; if you do, why not start working on something in your spare time? Why don't you start taking night classes in that subject that you've always loved? If you aren't happy with your current situation, one of two things has to change: your perception of the situation or the situation itself. The decision is up to you. Go out there, take risks and do something great with your life.

E.G.O.

Dealing with my ego is where I have struggled a lot and still do sometimes. An ego can ruin everything you have. It can destroy relationships, yourself, your own happiness and all of your possessions. An ego is simply a false sense of yourself and the world around you. People with egos tend to be curt and sometimes rude, thinking the world revolves around them, and they also seem to think that anything bad that happens only happens to them.

'Attitude is everything, so choose a good one.' This little affirmation is one that I learned from a guy called Wayne Dyre. I think it's an incredible affirmation, and it sums up 'Life Inside Out". If you can choose the right attitude, you can be or become whoever and whatever you want to become. Get rid of your ego and treat others with the respect that you want to be treated with. Be loving, caring and anything else that is positive. After all, the vibes you give out to the world are the vibes that you will get back.

Being *in to out* gives you the power and takes the power away from many circumstances. Life when lived this way is a beautiful place to be and it can allow you to experience everything from a more loving, forgiving and generous place. Becoming more loving, forgiving and generous has a ripple effect throughout your life. You will begin to see other circumstances through a different lens, and you will begin to be much more grateful. Being loving and caring is what we were always meant to be, but for a lot of us, somewhere in the years of growing up, our ego has taken over. This is not entirely your fault, as that is the way the world goes. I don't think it is true that the more things you have the more successful you are.

Having possessions can certainly be a sign of success, but success is a collaboration between many great things like hard work, giving back, gratitude, positivity and imagination. Learn to live life this way, and your world will change.

Mind, body, spirit

I believe we are three-part beings: mind, body, and spirit, and all three must be looked after.

Mind: I believe this is the most important part of us. Our minds determine everything that we do, say or experience. In order to look after the other two aspects of our life, I believe we first need to look after our mind. Our mind can be our most precious resource or our worst enemy. Looking after your mind is no easy task, but it most certainly is a task worth doing. Your mind will determine what your body looks like or feels like and your mind will also determine your spirituality. Your mind has the ability to make you into who you want to become. Give your mind the love and care it deserves, and live life from the inside out.

Body: I guess you've heard the saying, "Your health is your wealth". It is absolutely true, whether we mean our physical or mental health. In this instance we are talking about our physical health, but, again, good physical health starts in the mind with a decision to try and by looking at your physical health as a lifestyle and not as a chore. I believe each of these parts of our being feed into each other, and when you can gain mastery of one, you can gain mastery of the others that little bit easier. Getting yourself into good physical shape shows that you have the mental capacity to set a goal and work towards it. It's that simple. Look after your physical health like it's your child. Don't be so strict that your child feels controlled, but don't give your child too much room or it will go down the wrong path. Find a balance between enjoying yourself when you deserve it and being strict when you must be strict.

Spirit: The word spirit might lose a lot of people, and I don't want that. Spirituality to me is just being connected with the universe and has nothing to do with God, or Allah or any other supreme being. It is just about being in tune with the world and doing the things that serve the world. It is being mindful and connected with other people and the world around you.

I believe that there is a law of attraction at work in the universe – that when you take one honest step toward your goal or toward doing something great, the universe works to help you. Doors will begin to open that you never even knew existed, and you will come in contact with people that you once looked up to. This to me is spirituality. Take honest steps toward doing something great and the universe will guide you along the path of least resistance toward your dreams.

This leads me into living from a place of awareness. Living from a place of awareness is a form of spirituality. You feel connected to something that you may or may not want to label. You can attract anything you want into your life, and it starts by building a foundation. Being aware that a new foundation needs to be built in order to get rid of the old one, or being aware that there wasn't a foundation there to begin with, is the first step to changing your life. If you can live your life from a state of awareness, you can begin to see things about yourself that need to be changed and you can also see things about yourself that are absolutely beautiful. Both are as important as each other. You must also be aware that your values govern your behavior. This means that whatever you value, you will behave according to that value. If you love socializing, you will work all week and live for the weekends. If you become immersed in work, you will see work wherever you go, constantly checking e-mails and rarely taking the time out to slow down and reflect. Whatever it is, being aware will be the initial step to changing anything you need or want to change. Live life from the inside out.

❦

PETER CORNISH

Author and founder of Dzogchen Beara meditation centre

GANDHI'S QUESTION – 'How can I be the change that makes a difference?' – represents a flash of light from his culture. It indicates that the only effective way to achieve change is by changing ourselves and, thereby our actions. While the heroic work of groups like Medecins Sans Frontieres is both inspiring and vital, it is always a temporary fix. It's a selfless response to suffering, but it isn't enough to cure the background malaise of a species that has lost touch with its nature.

When we perceive a world of confusion, it's our own confusion we are confronting. In Gandhi's profound question it is *being* the change' that is crucial. When that is accomplished, a difference is spontaneously made.

Peter Cornish began his working life as an artist but after his sight deteriorated he gave up painting and began an in-depth study of Buddhism. In 1974 he moved to Ireland and founded the Dzogchen Beara meditation centre in West Cork, inviting Sogyal Rinpoche to be its spiritual director.

33

It is said that our innate nature is infinitely compassionate and wise. By working to return to that nature, we effect change on two levels. Outwardly, our actions will aid and motivate all those with whom we make contact. Inwardly, realising that the state of the world reflects the state of our minds, we'll attend to our housework and stop blaming others.

Whatever we believe, there are many ways of 'making a difference' but 'being the change' is the way to achieve it. While non-violent action against tyranny is essential, there are other ways than shouting at deaf politicians. Maybe it's time to drop our hypocritical pontification and live out the change in ways over which we have total control. Like...

Be the change that feeds the world.

If we change our attitude to our fellow beings, we might stop eating one another like this. By simply realising that all creatures have the same rights as this one, we'll relinquish the consumption of corpses. When we do, it is claimed, we'll become less aggressive. Certainly we'll help feed the hungry by increasing the productivity of available land. Certainly we'll decrease the output of greenhouse gas, so what the hell are we doing? We can't go on eating meat now that we know the harm that it does. Now that we know that each mouthful is stolen from someone who's starving.

If we have a serious addiction to flesh we might cut it out, for a start, twice a week. That would be a great outward example of 'being the change'.

And it's not just about meat. Thanks to constant bombardment by hype from the foodies, our tastes are now thoroughly jaded. We need to liberate our taste buds from control of the salesmen and women. I recently heard about somebody's sandwich. Layer upon layer of ever more exotic ingredients. Don't they know that there's no shortcut to satisfaction via increasing indulgence? It's bad for the heart, bad for the planet and bad for the self-respect.

Don't they know that the simpler your tastes, the more joyful and nobler your life is?

When we cut down on excess we deprive ourselves of nothing but guilt. There is more food for the hungry and less damage to our little systems. After a week of reasonable feeding, one slice of good Irish soda bread with pure olive oil becomes a feast for the stomach and conscience. I dare you, go on, you will love it.

Be the change that pacifies the world.

Sometimes it's quite hard to believe that, after all this time, we are still ruled by our primitive instincts of greed and aggression. For a while, once we had released ourselves from full-time manual labour, it was thought we would have time to think about this and calm down. But, frightened by the prospect of superfluous freedom, we hurriedly invented this electronic jungle to hide in. Then, delighted with our new distraction machines, we got comfortably lost in the static.

When we cut down on excess we deprive ourselves of nothing but guilt.

Manipulated today by commerce and digital 'group-think', we blindly follow the trends to conform. Or the fashion to practice tasteful rebellion within limits specified by the threat of a knock on the door. With silence like starlight gone from our cities, peace is some dream we dreamt in the past. Input and feedback go rattling around like peas in a drum bouncing off each other's projections. Deprived of the space to arise in, originality gives way to dull interaction as we grab each moment and stuff it with chat.

The only way we'll bring peace to our world is by establishing peace in ourselves. The constant flutter of electrical gossip corrupts what remains of free space. With our mindstreams reeling from irrelevant stories, and cameras recording our every move, we have no choice but to do what we're told; to obey our second-hand thought base, handed down from generations that got most of it wrong.

Or do we? Maybe it's time to turn off the telly, put our mouth to the headphones and start shouting 'stop'. Perhaps even get out in the silence and starlight and take a quick look at what's going on.

If we are to start changing our minds and the world, we need to think and take time to be without thinking. We need to un-plug the planet and go to the mountain that's always there in our minds. It's up to us to create the difference by dismantling the system we've established as 'me'. We need to relax and empower the amazing potential we have buried in gadget addiction. If even one day per week we switch off the noise to remember the value of stillness, time will expand and we won't miss a thing.

Then the easy awareness that we knew as a child might radiate in our action. It will calm the aggression that's activated in the scurry from thought to occurrence. It will deliver a feeling of joyous relief at the discovery that we *can* help – can actually help because we've understood that we ourselves *are* our surroundings.

Be the change that liberates the world.

So, being the change entails calming the mind. Once the mind calms it begins to experience freedom. Freedom to identify implanted concepts that have kidnapped unbiased awareness and are holding our insight to ransom. To help free the world we must first free ourselves from the habitual thinking that has chased us through ages and caused all this conflict between us.

The positive effect of the contemporary flurry of intense interaction is that a certain 'growing-up' is occurring. We are seeing the dangers of blind adherence to dogma. Accepting that our view is no more than our view, and extremism is any idea that we are right. We are rejecting out-of-date systems designed to keep us subservient to the priests and their princes. It was never the genius of those free-thinking misfits like Jesus and co that caused all the blood to be shed. They just spoke out and religions got founded. The purity of their message of love was perverted by churches fixated on power. Tribal instincts were skilfully nurtured to divide us as rivals for despots to rule. It's still going on, but there are signs that the young ones are waking while the rest of us stir in our sleep.

Being the change that will make a difference entails liberating ourselves from the personal dictators that govern our thinking. Reclaiming our minds is the only revolution that doesn't put one more tyrant in charge. By kicking out concepts we've taken for granted we can declare independence in the free state of the mind. We won't need a flag because flags imply borders and our new domain is open and free.

When this internal turning around takes place, our world will actually change. Assuming responsibility for all that occurs, our compassion will grow as we join the infinite dance. Having chosen simplicity, the grasping subsides and we become involved and detached and available like never before.

PAT *THE BARBER* CROWLEY
Author and speaker on self-inquiry

SPEAKING FROM a small attic loft in his daughter's house in a poor neighbourhood in Bombay, Sri Nisargadatta Maharaji, who died on September 8 1981 at the age of 84, spoke these words: 'Which world do you want to save? The world of your own projections? Save it yourself. My world? Show me my world and I shall deal with it myself. I am not aware of any world separate from myself, which I am free to save or not save. What business have you with saving the world when all it needs is to be saved from you? Get out of the picture and see whether there is anything left to save.'

For forty years people came from all over the world to spend a little time in his company; speaking only his native Marathi, he had

Pat Crowley, also known as 'The Barber', gives regular talks on spirituality and self-inquiry. In his book, *The Rose and the Stone,* he shows how coming to know our true nature teaches us that life itself, with all its joys and sorrows, is an expression of the divine.

no formal education nor book learning. He became enlightened in his thirties through direct self-inquiry and realised his true spiritual nature.

A collection of his talks were recorded and translated into English by a few of his European listeners. A short time after being rescued from eighteen years of active alcoholism I found myself reading the fruits of their labour, the collection titled *I Am That*. My childhood curiosity was turbo-charged back into wakefulness. I knew instantly and intuitively that this was the truth; the lifelong feeling of *Oops! Wrong planet!* that had been mine since childhood, took flight, as did my lifelong fear of life and death; this was the insight I had been searching for since the day I first emerged from the cradle. I had also sought for it at the bottom of every glass I had ever raised to my lips. Here was the answer, here was something I could do with immediate effect, and help ease my much troubled relationship with life, the world, myself, and my fellow human beings.

This was not a cosmetic exercise intended to change Pat for the better, no this inquiry went to the very heart of discovering who or what I really am, what exactly is born, lives, and dies. No more reliance and dependence upon second-hand information, no more living life with a second-hand head, taking shelter in believing or rejecting the thinking of others, whatever borrowed authority they may come dressed up in.

Intellectual understanding begins to rest in its proper place, in perfect partnership with intuition, our total intelligence, or whole mind, and the heart is released from the total eclipse of a much abused thinking process, and the homemade, man-made, thought-made, far-off Gods. Only then can all necessary changes happen automatically without effort or striving.

Many inspirational people have graced our blue planet Earth down through the centuries; they've helped bring about many changes for the better, and encouraged others to do likewise, yet, despite all the admirable progress on so many fronts, deep down within the heart of the human, little or no change has taken place. We are still competitive with one another, we are nationalistic, and emotionally, financially, sexually, and politically corrupt. We murder, maim and destroy others in pursuit of what we see as our entitlements, interests, and rights, and all of this can be traced directly back to one source: to a warped understanding of our individuality, beginning with the emergence in early childhood of ego, which brings the 'me' conviction – 'me' a person, an individual, separate and different from others, and apart from the natural world, which we view with trembling and suspicion (confined to a body that lives under a death sentence, something we learn to our horror). Into life we wander, living almost exclusively from within the narrow confines of thought and intellect, leaving our hearts, the centre of total awareness, intelligence and love, consigned to a the shadows, emerging only now and again whenever a faltering intellectual arrogance allows.

…this was the insight I had been searching for since the day I first emerged from the cradle.

Gandhi, Nisargadatta, and other sages knew well that surface changes can bring about only surface differences; to enact real, worthwhile change, one has to go deeper and understand intuitively and compassionately the true nature of what ails us, starting with one's self.

Let's listen a moment with an open heart to the wisdom of Krishnamurti: 'When you call yourself an Indian, or a Muslim, or a Christian, or a European, or anything else, you are being violent. Do you see why it is violent? Because you are separating yourself from the rest of mankind. When you separate yourself by belief, by nationality, by tradition, it breeds violence. So a man who is seeking to understand violence does not belong to any country, to any religion, to any political party, or partial system, he is concerned with the total understanding of Mankind.'

Now, just how do I achieve a total understanding of mankind?

Surely it is not possible without first gaining a total intuitive understanding of myself, such as asking the question: am I really just a little body, a little person, sandwiched between birth and death, totally separate from the rest of mankind, and the outside natural world? Can you see why this is so important, if any change within me is to make a difference?

Otherwise am I not propagating the very violence that Krishnamurti speaks of, and further engaging in misguided self-interest that Nisargadatta suggests is at the root of the problem?

And what of Gandhi suggesting that 'If we could change ourselves, the tendencies in the world would also change.' Surely Gandhi did not mean that by me changing my attitudes, or swapping one belief for some higher belief, all would change for the better? Because is it not 'Pat', with his slavery to ego and the bondage of self, who would do the improving? – the very one that needs improving in the first place? It's a contradiction, you see, and could not possibly bring about the difference Gandhi speaks of! Any changes brought about by thought alone cannot make a fundamental difference, at least not the kind that would allow you and I, the children of chance, a place to lay our much troubled and sorely abused heads. No, only a total, intuitive understanding of all that constitutes my humanity and person can bring about the kind of change that would make a lasting difference.

Why? Because it *is* the difference.

CLARE DOWLING

Novelist and screenwriter

YOU TRY not to say it to your kids but you invariably do on occasion: 'Eat your dinner, *please*. There are millions of people in the world with not enough food, and you're going to waste all that broccoli/cauliflower/pasta.' This obviously sunk in with my young daughter, who began to hold out her plate with the suggestion that we 'send it in the post to the hungry people.' And I'd have to explain that (a) nobody wanted her half-chewed broccoli and (b) the world didn't work that way. Her face would grow confused and a bit cross as I'd go on about the proper channels for making donations to those in need. But she would still persist in saving a quarter of her sandwich, or squirrelling away a bag of crisps for

Clare Dowling writes women's fiction, stage plays and television scripts. Her previous career as an actor provided inspiration for bestselling novels *Fast Forward* and *Too Close For Comfort*. Her television writing credits include *Roy* and *Fair City*. She lives in Dublin with her family.

43

someone she thought might be hungry. Eventually she found her calling with a shoebox appeal in school, where she was actually encouraged to post things to children in need, including sweets, which was clearly more satisfactory than cold broccoli.

Sometimes it does seem very complicated, the business of contributing something of yourself with the hope of it having an impact somewhere. The problems seem insurmountable.

Outrage is the enemy of apathy...If we get angry, it means we care, and then we'll do something about it.

Turn on the radio any day of the week and there's a new tyrant wreaking havoc on his people, or a looming food crisis in a country a lot of us might have difficulty finding on a map. It's difficult to imagine making a difference; and harder sometimes to make a connection.

I often think back to my teenage years, which I seemed to spend in varying degrees of outrage. I despaired over animal cruelty; was insulted over gender inequality and discrimination. You name it and I probably took umbrage. Going into my twenties I became a vegetarian, and a penniless actor who began writing feminist plays. At one stage I owned a pair of doc marten boots, which was the height of anarchy back then. I probably wasn't half the revolutionary I thought I was, but I was genuinely exercised about the state of the world, and not content to leave it go unchallenged.

That sense of outrage can pass, though, if we're not careful. As we get older, life gets in the way. There may be financial pressures, elderly parents, the school run. Time can be a problem. Worse, all that outrage from our youth doesn't seem to have made any difference at all; the world has just the same inequalities and injustices. There are still people in the world with not enough food to eat. Your cynical side begins to think, well, there's not much I can do at this stage.

Outrage is the enemy of apathy and finding it again is key.

If we get angry, it means we care, and then we'll do something about it. Certainly, there are no shortage of things to be outraged at; we just need to look outside ourselves, open our eyes and ears, and let ourselves appreciate just how outrageous some aspects of the world continue to be. When our young people and teens say, 'But it's not fair!' we shouldn't think them naïve; we should applaud them for their anger. We should join in their outrage; then we have the fuel for change.

MYLES DUNGAN

Broadcaster and author

HOW CAN I be the change and make a difference in the world?

I'd turn that around. How can anyone go through life and not make a difference? I'm not talking about profound Mandela-inspired revolution – agents of change like Nelson Mandela are rare and wonderful. But it is axiomatic that everyone effects change on the people and the environment around them.

That, for example, was the message from Clarence, the gentle angel in Frank Capra's glorious 1946 movie, *It's a Wonderful Life*. George Bailey, played by Hollywood's 'Everyman', James Stewart, contemplates suicide and reflects on what he sees as a wasted life. Clarence shows him otherwise, what a world

Myles Dungan has worked as a reporter for RTÉ radio and television as well as presenting a number of arts programmes. He is the author of many books, mainly biographies and histories.

without George Bailey would have been like. For a small but significant number of people it would have been radically different and considerably less agreeable. So never underestimate the influence of a single, unassuming person on the lives of those around him or her.

But when it comes to positive, societal change the best that most of us have to offer is a healthy scepticism and an inquiring mind. A simple direct question can often have far more power to effect change than a welter of uncompromising statements. 'Why does it have to be like this?' usually beats 'This is how it should be.' Because the follow-on question from 'Why does it have to be like this?' can be something like 'Why don't we do it differently?' That's more of an invitation, more inclusive than 'Let's do it this [my] way.' A pertinent question is the first step on the road to change. It's an expression of inquiry that invites a response, and opens a dialogue.

So I suppose the answer to the puzzle we started out with, *How can I be the change and make a difference in the world?* is actually a question. Typically Irish, answer a question with a question. The six most important words in the English language, and the most productive agents of change are … who, what, when, where, why and how.

Not that I'm being dogmatic about it or anything like that!

JOHN EVOY

Founder of the Irish Men's Sheds Association (IMSA)

IT'S A great honour to be invited to contribute to this book. By sharing some of my story and experiences I hope to, in some small way contribute to the powerful and essential work that the Hope Foundation is doing in protecting the children in Kolkata and creating lasting change in their lives.

I work with the Irish Men's Sheds Association and it's because of the success of the Men's Sheds Movement in Ireland over the past five years or so that my story is worth telling.

I think it is important and also sufficient to say that some years ago I went through a time in my life when I had very little motivation or enthusiasm for the joys of life. However, when

Best known as founder and CEO of the IMSA, John Evoy has developed a number of men's learning and well-being initiatives. He won the Social Entrepreneurs Ireland 'Impact' Award with IMSA in 2013, and in 2015 received a People of the Year Award.

I came to realise that life had more to offer, I found that it was not so easy to access the support that I needed.

Now, over twelve years later in my role with the Irish Men's Sheds Association, I have the task of making it as easy as possible for people to set up and run Men's Sheds. Men's Sheds are community spaces where men come together and work on projects and where they find meaning and purpose, friendship and belonging. They are spaces where men can find information about services and where they can find the mutual support they need to lead flourishing lives and to contribute fully to society.

There is a public perception that Men's Sheds are only for men who are struggling in life, perhaps faced with an issue such as isolation, unemployment or depression. And despite the fact that, in my opinion, almost all of us will experience some of these issues at some stage in our lives, Men's Sheds are for all men.

There are now over 230 Men's Sheds across Ireland with an estimated 7,000 men participating each week.

The one thing that Shedders have in common is that they have time on their hands and that they want to do something positive with that time. Of course, anyone experiencing the issues mentioned above are very welcome to a Men's Shed, but they don't come for that reason alone. They attend their Shed to share knowledge, experience, ideas, creativity and skills. The inevitable result is that great outcomes emerge. There are now over 230 Men's Sheds across Ireland with and estimated 7,000 men participating in their local Shed each week.

So what was my role in the development of the Men's Sheds Movement and how have I 'made a difference?' Men's Sheds are not my idea, nor was I responsible for setting up the first Sheds in Ireland. In fact Men's Sheds are an Australian concept and by 2009 a number of unconnected groups were establishing Men's Sheds here. The first was in Tipperary Town which was quickly followed by Sheds in Counties Meath and Louth and in Arklow in County Wicklow, and although I had been interested in Men's Sheds for a couple of years I was not involved with these early Sheds in Ireland. I had been working in community education with County Wexford VEC (now Waterford and Wexford Education and Training Board) with a focus on men in adult education, and in 2009, because of the work I was doing, I was invited to attend the Third Australian Men's Sheds Conference in Hobart, Tasmania. This trip was both a career and life changer for me. I met a couple of guys who were the drivers in the Men's Sheds movement in Australia, who were to become great friends and mentors to me and who in the long run have showed me what it really means to believe fully in something. They have also showed me how you can 'be there' for others while being at the other side of the world.

As well as attending the conference I visited several Men's Sheds in Tasmania, Victoria and New South Wales and returned determined to set up Men's Sheds here.

I remember clearly one piece of information about the development of Men's Sheds in Australia, which has impacted my work ever since; Men's Sheds had first evolved in Australia in the early 1990s and by 2005 there were about fifty Men's Sheds across Australia.

Then between 2005 and 2007 the Australian Men's Sheds Association was established and it was this development that led to the continuous and exponential growth of Men's Sheds. The number of Men's Sheds has doubled every two years since and there are now over 1,000 Men's Sheds in Australia. So I figured that it would make much more sense to put my energy into setting up an organisation to support the development of Men's Sheds across Ireland rather than focusing my energy on one or two Men's Sheds. This has proven to be the case and if a lesson can be learned from this, it is that we must think of scaling up from the very start of journey so as to have the biggest impact as possible. 'Think Big' as our great friends in Social Entrepreneurs Ireland say.

In the couple of years that followed I spent a lot my time travelling the length and breadth of the island, visiting the towns and communities where people had expressed an interest in setting up a Men's Shed. The number of Sheds grew and grew, as did the body of knowledge and experiences which would help to inform the best and easiest ways to set up Sheds. People often remark about how extensive my knowledge is when it comes to Men's Sheds but in reality none of it is of my own making. I have just been lucky enough to visit so many of the Men's Sheds and to hear so many great ideas that have created a well of information which I endeavour to distribute in every way I can. I think that's one of the symptoms of passion; telling anyone and everyone who will listen about your plans and ideas and about the impact that your work can have. At this stage some of my nearest and dearest need some 'Shed free' time and space when in my company.

So what difference has all of this made? I think it is very individual thing which can be explained much better by some of the men from the Sheds; some of the phrases I hear most often as I travel around Men's Sheds across the island of Ireland are that the Shed 'gives me a reason to get up in the morning', 'the best thing about this place is the camaraderie' or 'without this place I would be lost'.

We could use terms such as 'enhanced wellbeing', 'increased social capital' or 'improved community cohesion' but the simple fact is that when a group comes together and creates something positive for the community, then the outcomes are positive for everyone. Each group of men makes its own decisions about what activities to undertake and it is amazing how many of these groups choose to use their time and energy to do something positive for their communities, such as making benches for a local park or renovating old bikes for kids in their areas.

What difference have I made? Not a lot really, because every town and village has already got the resources to successfully set up and run a Men's Shed or most other community projects for that matter. In some cases people did need reminding of their capacity and ability. Our communities are full of the most amazing people that you will ever meet who care for and want the best for everyone in their communities. It's been great for me to be able to help in some small way and to have a job I love as a result.

To find out more about Men's Sheds visit www.menssheds.ie

MEIMEI FOX

Author, editor, and life coach

I'VE BEEN blessed with so much in this life. To begin with, I was born into a loving family, to parents who have always treasured me and put my welfare first. We never had to worry about having enough money to survive – we had food, shelter, clothing, all in plenty. I feel lucky to be American, enjoying tremendous rights and freedoms, while also appreciating the security my government provides. I received a wonderful education, and revelled in every moment of it.

But with those blessings comes great responsibility. I have always, since I was a child, felt a burning desire, a need, to make a positive impact on the world, to share the gifts I have been so lucky to receive in order to help

MeiMei Fox is the author, co-author, ghostwriter, and freelance editor of hundreds of health, spirituality, and psychology books, articles, and blogs, including *New York Times* bestsellers *Bend, Not Break* with Ping Fu and *Fortytude* with Sarah Brokaw. She also works as a life coach.

others. However, I haven't found one clear path for giving back. I volunteered at various non-profit organisations; I tutored and counselled under-privileged kids; I took my sweet Golden Retriever to visit elderly people in nursing homes; I donated money to causes I supported. Still, no single activity, cause, or project fully captivated my interest or attention.

I have always, since I was a child, felt a burning desire, a need, to make a positive impact on the world.

That all changed in 2004, when I stumbled upon HOPE Foundation on a visit to India. I knew at once that HOPE offered me a way to making a lasting difference. Touring the Girls' Home and visiting the slums of Kolkata with HOPE's medical team left a profound impression. The children I met had next to nothing in terms of food, shelter, or education; many had no families. Yet even living in extreme poverty with few opportunities for advancement, they showed such joy. A smile, a hello, a handshake, a photo on my digital camera – they returned every gesture I offered with utter delight. I felt inspired.

Since then, I have sponsored a child through HOPE and assisted the organization in any way that I can to get the word out about what they're doing to change the world. I love how my sponsorship of Rama has allowed me, for nearly a decade, to connect in a very real and concrete way with my desire to make a difference. If I were simply to write a check to the foundation each year, I'd certainly alleviate some of my privileged guilt. But I wouldn't be able to feel in my heart the truth of how my actions are helping another living being.

Thanks to HOPE Foundation, my 'adopted daughter' Rama sends me a handwritten card and a photo of herself each year. I look forward to these notes with the anticipation of a child on Christmas morning. I love hearing about Rama's studies, seeing her English language and writing skills improve, watching her grow up into a mature young woman in her photos year after year. No matter what else I might accomplish in terms of my career and my personal life, I know that I have changed Rama's life for the better. I have offered a girl who, at age nine, was nearly sold off the streets into sex slavery, a chance to become her best self. Because of HOPE, and my small contributions, Rama can dream. She can go after her dreams. And she can make of her life whatever she chooses. It is a truly glorious feeling for me to be able to support her in that.

After a few years of sponsoring Rama, I felt called to further serve the world by helping HOPE share its amazing projects with other Americans. Based in Cork, Ireland, HOPE isn't very well known in the US. I began blogging about my experiences as a visitor to the HOPE Girls' Home and sponsor of a child for the *Huffington Post*, as well as posting a great deal about HOPE on social media. Taking these actions has further deepened my commitment to HOPE, and also amplified my sense that I am doing my best to 'be the change'.

I admire Maureen Forrest, the founder of HOPE, deeply. Some people are meant for great projects, like starting and tirelessly running an international non-profit organisation that helps thousands of people every year. That calling may not be for me. But I have found my niche, a small way to contribute that gives me hope for a better world for us all.

VANESSA FOX O'LOUGHLIN

Publishing consultant and literary scout

DESPITE THE fact that I am the world's worst mathematician, the chaos theory or butterfly effect has always resonated with me – that the movement of a butterfly's wings on one side of the world can influence the formation of a hurricane on the other side of the world. When I look over the various things that have happened in my life, and the lives of others, I see this manifest in many, many different ways.

About fourteen years ago I watched a news report about an earthquake in Afghanistan – a little girl in a red dress stood amidst the rubble of her home. I was a mum at home with a little girl not much younger than the girl on the TV, and this affected me hugely. I de-

A publishing consultant and literary scout, Vanessa Fox O'Loughlin founded the Inkwell Group, *writing.ie* – a writing resources website – and Kazoo Publishing Services. She is vice-chair of Irish PEN and the Irish and Eurozone adviser to the Alliance of Independent Authors.

cided I wanted to raise some money for the relief effort. I didn't have big corporate links or connections then, but I had a gang of enthusiastic friends who agreed to organise several bake sales, coffee mornings and fund raising events. One of the mums, Kya Lowens, hosted a coffee morning, and a writer called Sarah Webb came along. We'd met previously a couple of times, but got talking on this occasion, and through this event and others became good friends. I had just started writing fiction and her advice to me 'just keep writing' is the best I was ever given. The butterfly's wings were starting to flap.

Fast forward to 2006, I wanted to learn more about the craft of writing and, unable to attend the courses and workshops that were available at the time, I decided to start running my own one-day workshops facilitated by bestselling authors. Sarah was the person I contacted for advice, and Inkwell Writers Workshops was born, a company that was to become a fully-fledged publishing consultancy and to give birth in 2011 to *www. writing.ie*, Ireland's national writing resources website.

The simplest thing: a phone call, an introduction, can change someone's life forever, and it is up to us to be the architects of that change.

Inkwell's role is to bridge the gap between the writer, agent and the publishing industry. It brings professionals together with new writers to show them how to improve their writing and bring it to a publishable standard. We connect writers with people who can help them.

And as a result, we make dreams come true.

From almost the first workshop Inkwell writers have been getting publishing deals – Laura Jane Cassidy was one of the first with *Angel Kiss*, and as she sat in that same workshop, little did Hazel Gaynor know that she would be signing with a US agent and her Titanic novel, *The Girl Who Came Home,* would be fought for by publishers on the other side of the world. From the fabulous *Parnell A Novel* (The History Press) to Sarah Griffin's memoir of emigration *Not Lost* (New Island), to Louise Phillips's bestseller, Irish Book Award nominated *Red Ribbons*, Inkwell and now *www. writing.ie* have helped hundreds of writers to achieve their dreams. And it all started with a little girl in a red dress.

Changing lives changes the world, a little bit at a time. We can all change lives – we can pay it forward, use our expertise to assist others. The simplest thing: a phone call, an introduction, can change someone's life forever, and it is up to us to be the architects of that change whenever and wherever we can. It's up to every one of us to flap our wings.

TEENA GATES

Author, broadcaster, and motivational speaker

I WAS twenty-three stone and unable to walk when a consultant told me I was dangerously ill. For the first time in years I took responsibility for my weight issues and several months' later and four stone lighter I got the 'all-clear'. I felt incredibly grateful for life and was passionately looking for a way to celebrate it, when the Hope Foundation contacted me at 98FM where I was working, and asked me to make a trek to Everest Base Camp to raise funds for street kids in Kolkata. I went on to lose another six stone and successfully took on the challenge later that year, making it to Base Camp. I learned so much along the way; and not just about health, fitness, and the power of the mind. In the past I would have thrown

Teena Gates is an author, televsion presenter, radio broadcaster and motivational speaker. She has earned a reputation as an 'adventurist' after losing more than half her own body weight in response to a health scare, going on to travel around the world exploring the theme that 'we all have our mountains to climb'.

I believe that life is for living, for doing what you can and then doing a little bit more.

pennies in a pot or bought a ticket for a charity, but I never engaged in fund-raising on any large scale. As a journalist I knew something about the size of the world's problems and felt daunted by my helplessness to make any dent in that. After my brush with illness, I went on to raise tens of thousands of euro for a variety of charities, with the help of the incredible generosity of my friends, neighbours and even complete strangers. I was also fortunate enough to be able to bring awareness to many stories of heartache and hope. HOPE, I learned, stands for Help One Person Every day. I can't solve the world's problems and I don't try to. But I believe I can help one person every day; even if that's just to smile at someone in the street. I started out being grateful, I still am, and the more I try to say thank-you, the more things I have to be grateful for. Now I believe that life is for living, for doing what you can and then doing a little bit more. Now I believe I CAN make a difference. Hope has taught me that.

MARK PATRICK HEDERMAN

Benedictine monk and writer

WHEN ASKED 'how can I be the change
and make a difference in the world', two
things happen. We think of all those wonderful
people who have actually made a difference
– Nelson Mandela, Gandhi, Mother Teresa
of Calcutta, for instance – and those quota-
tions used to inspire us in that direction – 'Be
the change that you wish to see in the world'
(Mahatma Gandhi) or 'I cannot do everything,
but still I can do something; I will not refuse
to do something I can do' (Helen Keller), or
'It is always because of one person that all the
changes that matter in the world come about.
Be that one person' (Buckminster Fuller) –
and then we think of ourselves and say, 'Sorry,
you must have got the wrong number.' Most

Dom Mark Patrick
Hederman, OSB, Abbot
of Glenstal Abbey,
County Limerick, is
a Benedictine monk,
teacher, lecturer and
writer.

of us are too hopeless, too useless and too irretrievably selfish to become candidates for saving the world.

And yet, if we look around us, nature can teach important lessons in this regard. One small example: a useless ugly creature that makes a difference by doing the one and only thing it was created to do is the yucca moth. Small, pallid, nondescript, it blends with the anaemic surroundings where it spends most of its brief adult life. And yet this anonymous nobody performs a task that no other creature on the planet is able to do. Adorning the mouth of the female Yucca moth is a pair of long prehensile maxillary palpi which allow her to develop one of the most extraordinary partnerships the world has ever known.

Find out the job you are created to do, no matter how small and insignificant it may seem to be, and do it.

Before I describe the partnership which has lasted for more than forty million years, let me tell you about the equally uninspiring partner who makes up the other half of the equation. Perhaps one of the most useless and unprepossessing of creatures is the Yucca plant. A trunkless shrub you might call it. Its woody fibrous stems end in tufts of leaves stiff as swords with sharpened points. Coarse fibre from the stem could be used for cordage if you were really stuck, and the saponaceous matter contained in the root might be used instead of soup if you were on a desert island. Indeed, 'desert candle' is the name given to one species of the plant. 'Unfit for purpose,' the interview panel might be excused for concluding. And yet, this ungainly creature is the chosen partner of the Yucca moth. They are interdependent and cannot live without each other. The moth pollinates the plant in return for food and shelter for her offspring. Evolution has shaped them to perform their symbiotic dance.

The Yucca moth emerges at the time of the opening of the Yucca flowers. This window of opportunity lasts sometimes for less than a single night. If the business is done on the night in question the Yucca plant can survive. The pistil of each yucca flower ends in a three-lobed stigma which surrounds a central secret opening. Pollen must be forced down this stigmatic depression for fertilization to occur. Such is the crucial event enabling the perpetuation of all Yuccas in the wild. Without this moth, Yucca plants would be extinct.

Most insects brush pollen onto a plant's stigma incidentally while looking for nectar. Pollination happens accidentally. Yucca moths, as they say, put all their eggs in one basket. 'Ovipositing' is the name of the game. Pollination, for them, is a hole in one. Nothing is left to chance. The moths roll the pollen into a ball under their chins. They climb the pistil and pack the pollen into the secret chamber. The plant can be fertilized by no other insect and the moth can fertilise no other plant.

How can I be the change and make a difference in the world? Find out the job you are created to do, no matter how small and insignificant it may seem to be, and do it.

Envoi

God, thou great symmetry,
Who put a biting lust in me,
From whence my sorrows spring,
For all the frittered days,
That I have spent in shapeless ways,
Give me one perfect thing.

TOM HICKEY
Journalist and blogger

A FEW YEARS ago, after much prodding, I started a blog. My first post was about reaching the ripe young age of 60, and the pressure from my family to write my story. You would think that after a lifetime in newspapers I would have jumped at the chance sooner, but in truth I was intimidated by the thought of putting myself out there before a public who might not be interested. The fear of failure is a powerful motive to do nothing. For whatever reason, I penned that first blog.

There was a moderate enough interest and some encouragement. A couple of people even started to follow the blog, which was very gratifying. Days later I was trying to tease out what I should write for my next

Tom Hickey worked as a sub-editor with the *Irish Examiner* until retiring in 2015. He writes a blog at *hickeysworld.com*, in which he discusses, among other things, facial disfigurement, having been burned in an accident as a child.

69

blog when I thought why not explain my facial disfigurement. It might just reach someone who was struggling to deal with their own disfigurement.

'Facial Disfigurement: a voyage Around My Face' was written in about forty minutes, and with the aid of an accompanying picture of my face, I told the story of how I accidentally set fire to myself, explained my injuries and the reconstruction work that followed, and tried to give a flavour of how I had struggled to deal with the psychological effects. I expected some reaction, but not the overwhelming support that followed. My phone started pinging with messages on Twitter and Facebook. People were sharing or retweeting the blog all evening and the following day. Trying to respond to comments was not easy because there were so many.

By opening up about my past... in as honest a way as I can, I hope that in some small way it will make a difference.

Among those who contacted me were friends who either never understood the mental anguish I had gone through, or colleagues who always assumed that I had dealt with my issues. Many also said that while they had known me for years they had never heard my story. Remarkable. I was also touched by some lovely messages from nieces and nephews too young to ask questions about my face, but glad they now knew the reason.

But it was the e-mails, letters and later phone calls from others with facial scars that touched me the most. These were people who had endured physical pain and emotional distress, some still not totally at ease with their physical selves. Like me they often had a difficult time dealing with people staring at them, making snide remarks and calling them names. Social isolation was often the only way they could deal with living, and I understood that. After all, I too had hidden part of myself away from others for many years, so successfully that they were unaware of how often I cried out of loneliness, and yearned for a girlfriend.

I could empathise with them, and I explained how I eventually reached a point where I knew I didn't want to be alone and needed to do something about it before it was too late. I did, and eventually met my wife Trish. We are married thirty years now and have two children, Daire and Sarah Jane. I had found a happiness and contentment I had only dreamed of through sheer willpower and doggedness.

My message was that they could also reach a better place in their lives by being positive, learning to ignore disparaging comments hurled in their direction and deal with those who stared at them. I dealt with self-loathing, humiliation, diminished self-worth, fear of meeting people – especially in crowded places like pubs and dances where you felt everyone was looking at you, even if they weren't.

Of course some of those who contacted me and had scars had adapted very well and were remarkably well adjusted. I was delighted for them.

One of the most surprising aspects of the reaction was the many who got in touch because my story – and some of my other blog posts – resonated with them. They were recovering or dealing with cancer, mental illness, family bereavement, or serious illness. All said they were uplifted and inspired by what I had written, which was immensely gratifying.

In my blog (*www.hickeysworld.com,* if you want to take a look) I mainly deal with issues in my life, from facial disfigurement to the life and death of my son Alan who had spina bifida. There is a lot of sadness there among those posts, but always I emphasise the bright side of life. By opening up about my past and doing so in as honest a way as I can, I hope that in some small way it will make a difference to someone and encourage them to deal with their own pain and perhaps be more positive in their outlook.

CON HURLEY
Journalist, life coach and author

Watch your thoughts; they become words. Watch your words; they become actions. Watch your actions, they become habits. Watch your habits, they become character. Watch your character, it becomes your destiny. – Frank Outlaw

I WANT to clarify the question I have been asked to address: 'How can I be the change and make a difference in the world?' As I see it, this is *not* a wake-up call for me to change and make a difference. Nor is it for anyone else. The fact is that everyone in the world, including me, is an agent for change and makes a difference whether or not we realise it.

This was brought home to me in July of 2013, when Eleanor and I celebrated our for-

Con Hurley worked as dairy editor of the *Irish Farmers' Journal* for 33 years before embarking on a new career as a life coach and giving courses on life topics and lecturing on the MBA programme at UCC. He is the author of two books: *Yes I Can*, on achieving personal succes, and a biography, *The Life and Times of Noel Murphy.*

tieth wedding anniversary. We had a very enjoyable gathering of family and close friends and we received many congratulatory cards. Two cards in particular stood out.

One was from my married son: *'You are an inspiration to us.'*

The other was from my niece and her husband: *'You're such a wonderful couple, we hope to emulate what you've achieved in your marriage.'*

Both messages are a clear reminder that the way we behave has an influence on those around us, our children, the society we live in and ultimately the world. It gave Eleanor and me great satisfaction to know that, through our marriage, we are a positive influence to our son Jerry and to Ailísh and Richard – their words are precious.

On reflection, I went back to the words that Eleanor and I exchanged forty years ago: *'I Eleanor/Con take you Eleanor/Con to be my lawful wedded husband/wife, to have and to hold from this day forward, for better, for worse, for richer, for poorer, in sickness and in health, 'till death do us part. So help me God.'*

More precious words. In addition we exchanged many other words before our marriage and in the years since. Some of the most important ones are: *love, respect, commitment, forgiveness, understanding, sharing, listening, care…and many more.* Many of these words remain unspoken, but they are in our heads and hearts as an agreement to building and sustaining our strong marriage as best friends and lovers.

Words, in fact are at the root of all human behaviour. Not just the spoken word, but the written word and the words we form when we think. Words begin life as thoughts in the head and are then transferred to others by mouth and pen. History is littered with the effects of spoken and written words, and, in my opinion, while speeches can rouse emotions in listeners, it is written words that have had the greatest effect on the history of mankind.

Think of the Bible, the Koran and the Vedas and the world religions they spawned – Judaism, Christianity, Islam and Hinduism respectively. Then think of the consequences of *The Communist Manifesto* by Marx and Engels, Hitler's *Mein Kampf* and Chairman Mao's *Little Red Book*. Countless millions of people have suffered and died as a result of the words in these books. The words of the great philosophers and writers have also had a huge, generally positive, influence on the social and intellectual evolution of humanity.

I do believe that the words (and thoughts) I use contribute hugely to how I see the world and how the world, and the people in it, sees me. There's a great example on YouTube about a blind man begging on the street and a sign in front of him saying: 'Please Help, I'm blind.' People pass by but very few put any money into his tin can. Then a woman takes the sign and writes something different on it, after which the money just flows in. What did she write? Simply, 'It's a beautiful day, but I can't see.' It is a perfect example of *'change your words, change your world!'* (You can see the video at *https://youtu.be/Bq3Dgy3Wx_0*).

Everyone of us possesses the power to influence change through the words we think, speak and write...

Every one of us possesses the power to influence change through the words we think, speak and write. I believe that most of us do not realise how much power we have and the care that is needed to choose the words we use. For example, take gossip. This is usually assumed to be harmless chit-chat about trivial matters, and it often is.

However, gossip can be very harmful. It can destroy reputations and create tremendous distress. I believe that society and the world would be a far better and safer place without the harmful and malicious use of words in gossip. Gossip is usually based on rumours, assumptions and beliefs that masquerade as facts.

This brings me back to what Gandhi said: 'Be the change that I want to see in the world.' And, whether I like it or not every day I am changing the world through the way I behave, the example I give and the words I use. As I look ahead, I will continue to live my life following Gandhi's advice. And the change I want to see is to see more and more people becoming aware of the power of the words they use and to use that power to create love, harmony, great relationships, peace and prosperity.

How will I do this?

Well, back to Gandhi again, I must start with myself and 'be the change'. Here are some of the ideas and principles I put into practice in my everyday life.

Firstly, I choose and select the words that I allow enter my mind. I don't want to be like Ramona about whom Bob Dylan's song said; '*I can tell your head has been filled with worthless foam from the mouth.*'

In practice this means being very selective about what I read, watch and listen to from external and internal sources. Obviously, this means TV, radio, internet and people I interact with. Less obviously, it means the conversations and voices that go on in my head. I am a great believer in positive thinking and guarding against negative thoughts.

Secondly, I select carefully the words I use when communicating with others through speech and writing. I know that they influence people so I do my best to use words that are constructive and help people and avoid those that could cause offence and harm.

Both of these choices are under my direct control. However, I have far less control over the words that other people use. Words, once spoken or written, are difficult to take back. However, they can be challenged – and this is the third way I endeavour to be the change I want to see in the world. Let me expand.

The verb 'to be' is a verb of certainty. Used properly it denotes factual information. For example the following are statements that can easily be checked against the facts.

It is raining.

She was married yesterday.'

However, 'to be' is widely misused to represent opinions and assumptions as facts.

For example:

It is an awful bad day today.

She wasn't a happy bride.

These are not facts, but interpretations of the facts. The first is fairly harmless. However, the second, which is both an assumption and an opinion, can be very harmful and lead to malicious gossip. So, before I say anything that needs consideration, I ask myself three questions:

Is it true?

Is it necessary?

Is it kind?

And then, I follow the maxim: *If you can't say something good about someone, don't say anything!* This is a really good test to use before you engage in gossip or loose talk. Buddha put it this way: *'Better than a thousand useless words is one word that gives peace.'*

I believe it is very important to distinguish facts from assumptions, beliefs and opinions. All of these are perfectly legitimate in communication – as long as it is clear that they are not facts. Far too often people forcefully express their opinions, assumptions and beliefs as statements of fact. I have been training myself to be able to distinguish one from the other and, when necessary, to intercede and challenge. I am also training myself to recognise when I am presenting opinions, assumptions and beliefs as facts, whether it is when conversing with others or myself.

The latter is not easy as most of them have become deeply embedded in my mind and I can effortlessly say things and make decisions without fully evaluating from where the information is coming. I find that I need to increasingly become aware of what information I base my statements on.

Self-awareness is a vital skill that I am finding difficult to learn and to implement. Difficult but not impossible. So, in examining my thoughts, decisions and what I say to other people I am trying to install the following questions as a thinking habit:

What are my assumptions?

Is this my opinion or internal belief as opposed to a fact?

This is relatively easy to do when writing but far more difficult during an active conversation, when I can get lost in the cut and thrust of a debate. I am getting better though at observing myself during a conversation by mentally standing back and examining what I am saying before proceeding.

Kind words do not cost much. They never blister the tongue or lips. They make other people good-natured. They also produce their own image on men's souls, and a beautiful image it is. – Blaise Pascal

RICHARD KEARNEY
Philosopher and author

LET ME begin with a story. In the 1980s, at the height of 'the Troubles in Northern Ireland, I was invited as a young professor of philosophy in Dublin to go to Derry, a very divided city at the time, and moderate a workshop between republican and loyalist ex–paramilitary prisoners. During the workshop, one of the republican prisoners told of how one night he was asleep in his bed when a group of loyalist gunmen broke into the house, bound and gagged him, threw him into the boot of a car, and drove him to a barn outside Derry.

They strapped him to a chair, and he was about to be shot. When he asked if he could smoke a last cigarette, his captors consented

Richard Kearney is the Charles Seelig professor of philosophy at Boston College, Massachusettss. He is the author of more than 20 books on philosophy and literature (including two novels and a volume of poetry). His most recent book is *Reimagining the Sacred: Richard Kearney Debates God.*

and gave him one. As he smoked the cigarette, he told the story of how he had become involved in the republican armed movement, of how his grandfather had been brutally tortured and assassinated, of how his father had been incarcerated, of how his mother had had a nervous breakdown and become an alcoholic, of how his brother had been knee-capped and maimed for the rest of his life. And he went on until he finished his cigarette. Then he waited for the gun to go off. But it didn't. There was no sound. No movement. He waited for five minutes, ten minutes, fifteen minutes, twenty minutes – still no sound. Eventually, he managed to free himself and looked around. There was nobody there; the barn was empty. And he walked home.

When he had finished speaking in the workshop, another man, a loyalist prisoner, stood up and said, 'I was that assassin. And I would have shot you. But I couldn't shoot you because, when I heard your story, I realised it was my story.'

I was very struck by this incident, by the impossible hospitality and empathy that had transpired in that exchange. And so a number of years later I set up the Guestbook Project in Boston College, where since 2009 we have been organising a series of interdisciplinary conferences, publishing books and journals and, most recently, establishing an international blog-site focusing on the theme of hosting the stranger: a theme based on the fact that, in most European languages, the word for 'guest' and for 'enemy' is the same – e.g., *xenos* in Greek, *hostis* in Latin – giving rise to 'hostility' and 'hospitality', both from the same root. The purpose of the project is to try to understand how, why and when this improbable act of hospitality can take place, when cycles of enmity can give rise to that miraculous moment of hosting the stranger.

A second story that has informed the Guestbook project is that of 'chancing your arm'. This goes back to 1492 when a great civil war was raging in Ireland and the Earl of Kildare, Gearóid Mór FitzGerald, hounded and eventually besieged James Butler, nephew of the Earl of Ormond, in St Patrick's Cathedral in Dublin. At one point FitzGerald said to himself, 'This must end. This endless cycle of blood-letting and vengeance can't go on.' He asked Butler to carve a hole in the door and said: 'I'm going to take off my armour and stretch my bare arm through, and you can either cut it off or you can shake my hand. If you cut it off the war continues. If you shake my hand, the war ends.' FitzGerald 'chanced his arm', Butler shook his hand, and the war ended.

These two stories are about the improbable act of the enemy becoming the guest. And what we are trying to do with Guestbook is to extend the programme beyond an academic scholarly exchange to a more global initiative where we invite young people from different sides of divided cities and communities throughout the world – Derry/Londonderry in Northern Ireland, Mitrovica and Vukovar in the Balkans, Jerusalem in the Middle East, Bangalore and Dokdo in Asia, Nairobi and Mozambique in Africa – to engage in a work of creative imagination, whereby instead of repetitively acting out the divisions of the past they make and re-make history as story.

Using basic phone cameras and free editing software, young people, as only young people of this generation can, break the cycle of trans-generational wounding and revenge by making short movies, several minutes long, in two stages. The first, where they exchange their respective narratives of hurt and hostility; and the second where they reinvent together, from the ingredients of their divided histories (Battle of Kosovo, the siege of Derry, the fall of Jerusalem) a new story, set in contemporary times, where the old cycle of violence is transformed and overcome. The aim is to encourage young people to chance their arms by retelling their narratives, and then make that impossible leap of hospitality, trust and imagination towards the possibility of something new.

For more information about the Guestbook Project, visit www.guestbookproject.com

KATE KERRIGAN
Novelist and newspaper columnist

PHOTO: NIALL KERRIGAN

I THINK that making a difference is not about grand giving gestures but simply living a good life.

I remember a number of years ago a friend of mine lost her father and, although I did not know the man well, the fact that there was standing room only right through the car park at his funeral told me all I needed to know.

There were eighteen priests squashed onto the tiny altar and from that alone I surmised he must have been an extraordinary man. From the few times I met him I could tell he was an impeccably mannered old-school gentleman – like my grandfather: a devout, respectable, pioneer who used his intelligence to do good things for people. A decent man. And

Kate Kerrigan is the author of six novels, one of which, *Ellis Island*, was a *New York Times* bestseller in 2013. Her most recent work is *The Lost Garden*. She also writes a weekly column in the *Irish Mail* about her life in Killala, Co Mayo, and contributes to RTE's *Sunday Miscellany*.

so I grieved, not just for Paul Leonard and his family, but for the quality of generosity, decency, the uncompromising practice of Christian values that marked out extraordinary men of that generation.

Today, we aspire to mark ourselves out as extraordinary by being thinner, richer, having better cars, and bigger houses than our neighbours. 'Goodness' is not an achievement.

'Decency' is not acknowledged as a quality. Last year, Vincent, my grandmother's next-door neighbour, died, but not before he had cut enough turf to see his widow through the following winter.

Her cousin John, when he knew he wasn't going to see Christmas, bought and sent all of his Christmas cards in November. Mindful of others, in the small ways that matter, right to the end.

It is depressing to think that the very qualities that mark us as outstanding human beings ...have become so unfashionable.

Are there still compassionate auctioneers like my friend's father who can be trusted to look after the affairs of their elderly and the needy clients? Men with humility who are never boastful or flashy although they might have reason and means to be both? And while I was sitting in Killala church listening to Paul's eulogy I thought: is this the last generation of this kind of 'ordinary' yet extraordinary men?

What will they be saying about my generation of high achievers – 'He had wall-mounted flat-screen TVs in every room and a Lamborghini by the time he was 50. He upgraded his house and his wives six times in a lifetime?'

It is depressing to think that the very qualities that mark us as outstanding human beings – self-sacrifice, kindness, generosity of spirit – have become so unfashionable, so dwarfed by modern passions of glamour and instant gratification.

I then looked at the front pew, which was filled with Paul's children, and I realised that they all have at least one thing in common – a social conscience. They are all, in one way or another, involved or interested in some kind of social or community activism.

Paul Leonard's legacy of decency is in his children, how they live their lives and what they pass on of that to their children.

So even in these selfish times, it's still possible for parents to hand on a strong moral legacy, if we are willing to mark ourselves out from the pack.

Through the values that we instill in the next generation we can make a difference not just in our own lifetimes – but in theirs too.

CHUCK KRUGER

Author and poet

AT MIDNIGHT I heard a rapping on the front door and called out from around the corner in the living room, 'Come on in! *Herein, bitte!*' It was middle of February, 1992, a little over a month before our move from Switzerland to Cape Clear, Ireland.

In stumbled a swarthy post of a man. His blotched face, covered with grey stubble, jerked about in multiple tics. An extraordinary stench filled the house. He was breathing fast, almost gasping. We'd never seen him before.

We motioned him to sit down, quickly discovered German our language in common. He'd once worked as kitchen help on a German train. His name was Mislim. Did we know where he could spend the night?

Chuck Kruger lives on Cape Clear Island off the south-west coast of Ireland with his wife Nell (pictured with him above). He is a regular contributor to RTE's *Sunday Miscellany,* has published a number of volumes of poems and recently completed his memoirs, *Moments: A Miscellany of Memories.*

When we learned he was a Yugoslav, we suggested he cross the road and talk to some of his fellow countrymen, our only neighbours, who lived in a tiny barracks and performed seasonal road work and gardening. The five of them paid 200 Swiss francs a month per bed to the company that employed them.

Ah, but our guest had already talked with our neighbours. It was they who had suggested he come see us. We'd once helped one of them obtain free medical attention from a doctor friend, so naturally we could help this man too. They regretted that he couldn't sleep in the barracks because if they were caught housing an unregistered person, they'd be thrown summarily out of their jobs – and out of the country.

Slowly we pieced together Mislim's story. He'd hitchhiked non-stop for the last four days from a little village in Yugoslavia. He hadn't slept save in snatches. He'd no passport. He'd crossed all borders illegally. To enter Switzerland from Italy he'd hiked mountain passes at night. He'd no belongings with him, no money. Truck drivers had given him lifts.

We carried a mattress down, made up a bed in the living room. Because of our forthcoming move to Cape, the upstairs bedrooms were stuffed with banana boxes, the beds dismantled. As he drank his tea he talked.

Two weeks earlier he'd been father of six happy children and grandfather to one. But sectarian fighting had broken out in his region. One of his sons, a captain in the Bosnian army, had been ordered to fire upon a crowd; when he refused, he was immediately carted off to prison. Mislim's wife couldn't stop crying. When she went to the prison to visit her son, the young man wasn't there – he'd been shifted to the prison hospital. When she got there, the police refused to let her see him. Torture, she imagined.

Mislim's eldest daughter had been in a crowd indiscriminately fired upon. Because she gave assistance to one of the wounded, she was taken off to prison after first being machine-gunned in the legs. That'd teach her to interfere with justice. Another daughter had been thrown in prison for reasons unknown. All in the last two weeks.

To get these three children out of prison he needed to raise money quickly, 1000 Swiss francs to hire a solicitor, another 1000 to pay the customary bribe to the judge. The only place to raise such sums, he knew from his experience aboard German trains, was well-heeled Switzerland. Here he was. Could we help?

During the next week Mislim slept in our house. One day I took him to an English-speaking international school where I'd friends and helped him relate his story to the advanced history class. Current affairs live. As further horrendous details of atrocities committed in his region came out, students became sceptical. So too the teachers. The international press had, at this point, carried next-to-nothing about the turmoil in rump Yugoslavia. Surely it was preposterous, then, to think that an enlarged family of ten, in the heart of Europe, didn't have, for example, enough milk to last another week. Don't bother us with melodrama.

...she was taken off to prison after first being machine-gunned in the legs. That'd teach her to interfere with justice.

But the school, which catered to the children of multinational executives, said, 'Have no fear, we'll help out.' After several meetings, it gave Mislim 100 Swiss francs. But, cautioned the headmaster, maybe it was all a scam. I hadn't thought of that. I'd watched Mislim forget to breathe.

I called several churches. A tiny Baptist church where I had a minister friend, a German who also travelled Eastern Europe for Amnesty International, raised 300 pounds. He recognised the story as authentic. No questions asked.

I gave Mislim addresses, telephone numbers, cash, and he began visiting churches in other parts of Switzerland. He travelled discreetly, underground, worried that the police would nab him.

The more we heard from him, and the longer he lived off and on with us, the more we knew he was genuine. That he wasn't the genuine article, in fact, had never entered our heads until we tried to 'touch' people other than ourselves. We helped him wire hard Swiss francs to the solicitor.

Mislim's tics didn't improve. He still caught his breath before every sentence, every phrase. We worried that he'd gag. He'd so fixated on his family's suffering that he didn't, couldn't, think of himself. We made him eat.

One day, through a chain of telephone calls, he learned that, at last, at least, his eldest daughter had been freed. He'd paid over 1100 Swiss francs to the judge and solicitor before effecting the release.

We haven't heard from Mislim since he set off to hitchhike back to whatever was left of his family and his village. He was 53 years old, my age then exactly, a Muslim convinced that Karadzic and Milosevic would deprive him of all he loved but determined not to die until he had given every ounce of himself to his loved ones' plights. What else, finally, is there to do?

Two weeks after Mislim left, and we had completed our move to Cape Clear, we could still smell his presence as we unpacked the banana boxes. It was the perfume, we realised, of suffering.

And now, twenty odd years later, we can't forget how one single solitary sacrificing person changed how we look upon this still sadly war-torn world, to which we need to give something of ourselves if there's to be any hope.

MARY MALONE
Novelist

CONTEMPLATING ON how an ordinary person like me can be part of change and make a difference in the world provides an ideal opportunity to assess the role I (or indeed any individual) can play in introducing change in society and how our endeavours can improve the world we live in and make it a kinder place for everyone.

Our chance in life hinges predominantly on luck, beginning with the type of family we are born into, the neighbourhood we are brought up in, the people we strike against and befriend (or who befriend or abandon us), the educational chances we receive, how hard we choose (or not) to work if we're given opportunity and above all the decisions we make

As well as being a novelist and freelance journalist, Mary Malone works fulltime in the Central Statistics Office. She has had five novels published, the most recent being *Where There's A Will.*

as we go through life and our ability to cope and start over when plans go astray or we're faced with adversity.

Accepting our fate or fortune (good or bad) may sometimes feel overwhelming and outside of our control. And my experiences are modest when compared with other races and creeds. So what can I do to help those less fortunate? How can I be part of 'change' for others?

I can express kindness and understanding to all those I come across – family, friends, acquaintances, colleagues. I can donate a little of my time to the elderly or vulnerable in my neighbourhood. I can be more observant and instead of walking on by when I notice a young mother dragging a buggy up steps or an elderly person struggling with shopping, I can display kindness and concern and stop and offer help.

Change can be exciting. Change is opportunity. Change is rewarding. Being part of implementing change is an honour.

I can make an effort to smile as I cross the street. All too often we forget how contagious a smile can be. I can remind myself that everybody likes to matter and feel important or at the very least feel included. I can remind others who appear fortunate to spare a thought for those more in need.

I can help make kindness and thoughtfulness the new 'norm'. I can publicise the value of the Hope Foundation and the real stories behind the advertising. I can apply the beliefs of the Hope Foundation volunteers nearer to home.

I can lead by example and seek out ways – big or small – to make a bigger difference. I can take pride in being part of The Hope Foundation initiative. I can talk about The Hope Foundation and ensure this worthy charity isn't forgotten between big gestures. I can inform my family, friends and neighbours of the hard work and diligence others are affording to those worse off. I can plant the seed in the minds of other people that every little helps and they too can make a difference.

I can promote the benefit of change. Change can be exciting. Change is opportunity. Change is rewarding. Being part of implementing change is an honour – even if it's the small task of writing this article and putting my name firmly and proudly behind the difference Hope makes to the neglected children of Kolkata.

These children, just like every one of us, are victims of the 'luck' (mostly misfortune in this case) they were afforded in life – the poverty they were born into, the cruelty and neglect they have been exposed to, the dangers in the societies they're brought up in. Let us support the magnificent difference being made by The Hope Foundation. Let us do what we can to expand their resources. Let us all join together to be part of change and ensure these children are brought more and more to the forefront, working to guarantee a minimum of basic human rights – education and healthcare – and helping them to be part of change themselves.

DAVID MCCARTHY

Human rights and mental health activist

I HAVE thought about how I would write
this piece for a while, thought about how I
would frame it and what I would say. I think
about our society and its place in history from
time to time; I wonder how we will be talked
about it in the history classes of the future.
It is hard for us to look at ourselves in the
'NOW' and to judge how history will reflect
how we lived our lives and the type of society
we allowed to develop. Will it reflect a time of
personal greed over community growth? Will
it reflect a time when intellectual pursuit was
shunned over wealth creation? Or will it show
a development in our social evolution through
social media that is equivalent to the revolution unleashed by Gutenberg in 1450?

David Mc Carthy
is a professional in
strategic planning and
organisation. He has
worked for human rights
in mental health, most
notably with Mad Pride
Ireland as well as with
campaigns for ending
the Direct Provision
system and other
abuses.

I wanted to frame this piece around how the structures we build around ourselves frame how we live our lives and how we interact with others. I have a slight obsession with the concept of monarchy, not just the British royals but of the remnants of this old world system all across Europe. I just can't get my head around monarchy as a concept and why citizens want to hold on to it. I was at a conference in Denmark a few years back where I had dinner with a group made up of Dutch, Swedish and Danish people so I asked them were they monarchists or did they feel it was an outdated institution? To a man and women they all felt that although flawed their royals had a place in theirs and their respective country's lives.

It not being the norm for me to be dining with a multicultural bunch of monarchists I followed this up by asking what place that was? This is where it got interesting as they all agreed that as heads of state the royals had a role as ambassadors for their country and cultures. I tried to argue that the presidents and other officials of their democratically elected government fulfilled this role and while they agreed they felt that there was still a place for their royals. Undeterred I asked why they were happy to pay taxes to a family who were not elected, could not be removed and were only there because of coercion, violence and force in centuries past. Now while they did feel that maybe they got too much money and that those outside of the king/queen and crown prince/princess should have to work like everyone else they all agreed that the institution of the monarchy should be fully maintained.

I was just as confused. Maybe it is because the Irish monarchic system was quashed so successfully by the colonial British, but I have no attachment to this concept or institution. I have spent a lot of time (not so much that it gets in the way of my life, I'm not that boring I swear) wondering what daily life is like for these royals. Do they truly believe they are God's appointed rulers etc and do they honestly believe that the terra firma and those on it are their possessions? Surely not, surely in 2015 they know what they are; a remnant of an ancient corrupt institution, essentially a posh mafia who have eked out a niche in the market for 'The Family'

So why am I ranting about royals in this conversation about where we are in our social evolution? Well it is because I would argue that we are living in a time of change just like the middle ages — a time of flux that will herald a new age of enlightenment. In the first millennium AD, we saw the end of the old empires and the birth of organised religion as a force in our daily lives. The second millennium saw the growth of feudalism and the harnessing of religious power for state/monarchy/family interests and control. Then we could argue that this, the third millennium should see the next step in our social evolution, and what will that be?

...we are moving away from physical community to virtual community...from social responsibility to individual advancement.

The end of each era saw a period where old systems die out and new ones are born. As a society we are moving away from physical community to virtual community. We are moving away from social responsibility to individual advancement. I am not arguing that this is either bad or good. I am simply saying this is a natural occurrence in our evolution as a species. I suppose like most things historic nostalgia adds a gilded view but I do feel that in times past we had a greater focus on the hero, the thinker and great ideas then we do today.

Now don't get me wrong, I realise that the development of the micro-chip and all things technological will be the driving force of our next social evolutionary step. I also realise that these developments will create a different society peopled with a different population who will be comfortable with all their surroundings. But I am being selfish, because I feel I am sitting in that middle period, I would prefer us to have heroes both intellectual and societal who are not just celebrities whose only talent is the ability to promote themselves.

Taking a purely Irish scenario, while we may have lost our royals many moons ago we have only in my generation removed the shackles of the Catholic Church as an overbearing force on our lives. So how can we in Ireland use this period of flux to herald in a new social order where the community and not the individual is key? The answer I think lies within the teaching of many of the organised religions existing today: those of love, care, sharing and support in a world of equality. Taking the good from Catholicism, Islam, Judaism, or any other religion, we have a starting point.

I am no fan of organised religion in any of its forms but I am a fan of love and humanity. So I would argue that if we all as individuals let our hearts be our Church, let our conscience be our gospel and let our humanity be our God then we can build a stronger, more beautiful and caring society to pass on to the next generation. The last century saw the change to democracy and this century is seeing the dilution of organised religion; both of these developments have led to an increase in the power of the individual. Forces like capitalism are fighting hard to corrupt this but if we all to a man or woman take personal responsibility to live our lives better, to help others less fortunate, to be less enamoured with personal greed and gain then we can truly build a better future.

So to conclude my meanderings, I am a believer in active citizenship and that is where I will try to have an impact – offline and in our communities, working to ensure that I keep the interests of others close to my own, to keep a balance between personal gain and the community around me. How can you be the change, well it is simple really. The next time you pass a homeless person think about buying them a sandwich or a coffee. The next time someone asks for help give it, if you know someone who won't ask, offer. Talk to yourself and your loved ones, share our joys, hopes and our fears. If we all do a little more of this then maybe we won't be looked back on by history as the 'Dark Ages' of our next social evolutionary leap.

HUGH MCFADDEN

Poet and journalist

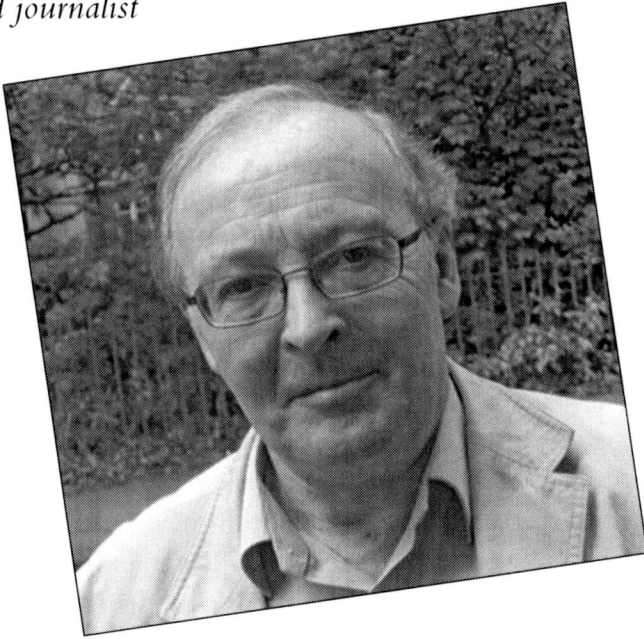

THE TWENTIETH Century was the most violent age in recorded history, with two world wars and the development of nuclear weapons which changed the entire nature of warfare and introduced the very real threat of the total destruction of the world and the annihilation of its inhabitants; ushering in the 'Age of Anxiety', the Cold War between East and West, and an unprecedented arms race that has changed the balance of power between nations, leading to attempts to create a 'Star Wars' anti-missile defence shield, the proliferation of nuclear weapons to a number of States, and the fall of the Soviet Union.

Rather than create the necessary conditions for peace to be established through de-

Hugh McFadden is a poet, critic, literary editor and journalist. His poems have been published widely in literary magazines and he is the author of four collections of poerty, the most recent being *Empire of Shadows* (Salmon Poetry).

tente and the fear of nuclear war, these developments have not prevented the continuation of 'conventional' wars throughout the latter decades of the last century, from Korea to Vietnam and the rest of what once was called Indochina, to several Mid-East wars, the Iran-Iraq War and a large number of local conflicts in Africa, Asia and even in Europe, with the Balkan wars and more recently the conflict in Ukraine. Since 2003 and George W. Bush's 'Shock and Awe' assault on Iraq, the United States has been engaged in continuous warfare across Afghanistan, Iraq, Somalia, Yemen, Libya and Syria, with both direct engagement by its troops and support for proxy armies. Israel, a nuclear power, has engaged in warfare in Lebanon and Gaza.

During this time the ability of the United Nations to stop armed conflicts and to maintain peacekeeping missions in troubled areas of the world has greatly diminished, as its influence has been severely undermined by the unilateral actions of some of the leading world powers who nominally pay ritual respect to the ideals of the UN, yet nevertheless conduct armed invasions of other countries and interventions in civil wars.

Last autumn marked the centenary of World War I which, at its outbreak, was hailed by much of the Western press as 'the war to end all wars': instead of achieving that result, the way the war was conducted with a demand for total victory and the capitulation of the Axis powers, along with the terms of the Treaty of Versailles, guaranteed the renewal of an even greater conflagration in the subsequent World War II only two decades later.

The need to promote a climate of nonviolence and to find international mechanisms for the resolution of conflict between states and within states, among communities of different ethnic origins, religious affiliations and cultural allegiances, has never been greater; even as the Western representative democracies led by the US and the EU attempt to combat resistance to their hegemony and control of energy sources and much of the wealth of global economies. The so-called 'War on Terror' has itself turned into a widespread war of terror. The attempt to project the shadow of 'evil' (fear) onto the foreign 'enemy', to demonise that enemy and to try to destroy it by military means, has led to the diversion of enormous amounts of money for an ever-growing arsenal of weapons. Recently, for instance, the US Congress has voted more than $1.5 trillion for the development of the F-35 Lightning II Stealth fighter jet plane; while in Britain there is considerable controversy over the enormous cost (as much as £100 billion) of replacing the UK Trident nuclear weapons systems, at a time when severe austerity cutbacks are being imposed on many budgetary areas, including welfare services and the National Health Service.

This concentration on militarism and the arms race has largely been accepted by much of the mainstream media as necessary for the defence of the West, both externally and internally, and a climate of renewed fear about the military intentions of Russia has been drummed up in the mainstream media since the recent conflict in Ukraine and the return to Russia, or annexation, of Crimea. But these fears and military build-ups, apart from swelling the coffers of the military-industrial complex, have achieved neither greater security nor peace of mind in the West. Opposition to these militaristic policies has come largely from such organisations as Pax, Pax Christi, Caritas, CND, NGOs linked to the UN and the Council of Europe, the International Federation of Red Cross and Red Crescent Societies, the International Peace Foundation, Amnesty International, Greenpeace International, some left-wing groups and, significantly, new social media contacts that do not rely on the traditional 'gatekeepers' of 'old' media.

Leading intellectuals in America and elsewhere, such as the MIT professor Noam Chomsky and the writer Gore Vidal, have

The need to find international mechanisms for the resolution of conflict…has never been greater.

poured scorn on the so-called 'War on Terror' allegedly being pursued by the US and its Western allies. Chomsky has pointed out that the incidence of armed violence, or terror, in the world has greatly increased since the invasion of Iraq in 2003, and that the US Intelligence services had predicted before the invasion that one outcome of that invasion would be such an increase in violence. What they did not seem to predict was that a completely new breeding ground would emerge across much of Iraq and northern Syria for groups such as Al-Qaeda and, after the debacle of intervention in Libya and Syria, IS/ ISIL.

Gore Vidal scornfully dismissed the notion of a 'war on terror' as being 'as idiotic as a war against dandruff', describing the terminology as a nonsense.

What, then, is the solution to this problem of armed violence and war in the world? If, like the present writer, one longs to see an end to organised warfare and, instead, the inauguration of an era of peace with justice to allow for the amelioration of poverty and an end to hunger and famine in the poorer and less-developed areas of the world, how should we proceed?

Some of the greatest minds of our age, including Albert Einstein, Mahatma Gandhi and the Trappist monk Thomas Merton ('Dom Louis') have grappled with these difficult problems regarding war and peace. Einstein is quoted as saying 'You cannot simultaneously prevent and prepare for war'; that peace cannot be kept by force, but only by understanding human nature and by mutual tolerance; and that 'nothing will end war unless the people themselves refuse to go to war', adding that he did not know with what weapons World War III would be fought, but that World War IV 'will be fought with sticks and stones' (after a nuclear holocaust).

'Mahatma' Mohandas K. Gandhi, known in India as 'Bapu' or 'Father of the Nation', led that great country to achieve independence from British colonial rule by pioneering non-violent political protest and civil disobedience campaigns through direct peaceful action. He believed that a kind of political or military victory attained by the use of violence was tantamount to a (moral) defeat, because it was bound to be temporary and temporal. He considered non-violent protest action to be the weapon of the strong, not the weak, and believed it was in the long run the mightiest weapon and the most effective.

But he also warned that 'the cry for peace will be a cry in the wilderness, so long as the spirit of nonviolence does not dominate millions of men and women'. Since he considered man to be the product of his thoughts, then 'what he thinks, he becomes'. The famous quote attributed to Mahatma Gandhi, 'We need to be the change we wish to see in the world', is probably a paraphrase of his view regarding the need of the individual who seeks peace and social justice to change his or her own character and habitual actions in order to achieve that goal of peace. The quote seems to have appeared first in print in an interview with Gandhi's grandson, Arun, conducted for a magazine article by the writer Carmella B'Hahn.

Gandhi instanced the life of the Russian writer, Leo Tolstoy, as a life which was 'devoted to replacing the method of violence for removing tyranny or securing reform by the method of non-resistance to evil'. He would meet hatred expressed in violence by love expressed in self-suffering – this being the divine law of love.

This elevation of love as the supreme virtue was echoed in his writing by Thomas Merton, who commented on the irony of a Hindu sage being the most profound exemplar to the West of the Christian Gospels' commandment of love as enunciated by Jesus Christ in his teaching, especially in the Sermon on the Mount. Writing on 'The Bomb and Nuclear Deterrence', Merton wrote of how so many in the West were walking backwards towards a precipice they knew was there, insisting all the while that they were going forward, and this because 'the world in its madness is guided by military men, who are the blindest of the blind', the new profession of nuclear strategists with their crazy eschatological messianism and pessimistic evaluation of mankind as exemplifying evil always in the 'Other', the 'Enemy'. The 'Bomb', he said, is the eschatological weapon *par excellence* for a weary, confused, world riddled with fear and more than half in love with the idea of the apocalypse of a nuclear war.

Gandhi, in contrast, advocated nonviolence, a nonviolence of the spiritually strong, as Merton understood it. In 'A Tribute to Gandhi' (*Thomas Merton on Peace,* 1971/ *The Nonviolent Alternative,* 1980), he wrote of Gandhi's visit in 1931 to England, where the ruling class still deluded itself that the British Raj was a purely benevolent, civilizing enterprise for which the Indians were not suitably grateful. Within a dozen years after Gandhi's visit to London, as Merton put it, 'there were more hideous barbarities perpetuated in Europe, with greater violence and more unmitigated fury than all that had ever been attributed to the despots of Asia. The Western allies did not want a renewal of world war in 1939, but they wanted a political and economic situation that made war inevitable. The British Empire collapsed. India attained self-rule. It did so peacefully and with dignity. Gandhi paid with his life for the ideas in which he believed.'

...the development of nuclear weapons had made the concept of a 'Just War' outdated.

The rest of the century was marked by chaos and struggle in countries that were once colonized, then by the Cold War between East and West, local wars in Asia, Africa, the Mid-East and Far East, and the gradual decline of the West as the pre-eminent economic and military power. The 21st Century has been marked by continuous warfare and a huge rise in what the West has termed 'terrorism', involving mainly Islamic jihadists and the armies of the Western powers.

In essays such as 'Man is a Gorilla with a Gun', and 'Faith and Violence', Merton tried to chart a way forward for the West which involved a renewal of Christian optimism that peace was possible, and he countered the prevailing pessimism of the militarist mind-set that continued to prepare for war, in a media climate that had as its motto 'bad news is good news'. In 'Breakthrough to Peace', he warned that the military strategists and political policy-makers believed that the key question now was not whether war can be avoided, but whether war can be kept within 'safe limits' – 'safe', that is, for the West. But the development of nuclear weapons had made the concept of a 'Just War' outdated.

Decisions on war, he reminded us, were moral decisions: and the 'enemy' is as human as we are, and not an animal or a devil. We have to be aware of the often hidden forces within us that dictate fatal decisions. We must learn to distinguish the free voice of conscience from the irrational compulsions of prejudice and hatred. We must be reminded of objective moral standards. Our problem is a moral and spiritual problem. We cannot think this way, he wrote, 'unless we shake off our passive irresponsibility, renounce our fatalistic submission to economic and social forces, and give up the unquestioning belief in machines and processes which characterizes the mass mind' – a mass mind easily influenced and manipulated via the mass media.

History, he said, is ours to make: 'Now above all we must try to recover our freedom, our moral autonomy, our capacity to control the forces that make for life and death in our society.' His admonitions were never more urgent and topical, as the West preaches the virtues of its purported freedoms, of speech, expression and assembly, while simultaneously restricting these very freedoms in the name of security and of the national interest.

Many of the then young in the 1960s in the West wanted to 'change the world'; some wanted revolution. Certain socio-sexual cultural changes did occur, but the longed-for political and social changes drowned in a sea of violence, drug-taking, self-indulgence, and escape from reality through addictions of all kinds that swept through Western society in the past forty or fifty years.

The most difficult change of all is to change one's own thinking and behaviour. The man or woman who achieves victory over himself or herself is greater than the man or woman who conquers a city. Gandhi understood that spiritual maxim; so, too, did Thomas Merton. Human rights and civil rights activists such as Martin Luther King Jr and Nelson Mandela also understood the need to base their actions on moral principles. Nonviolence was a principle that inspired all of them. In an age of ubiquitous war and violence, we need to return to this key human principle. As Bob Dylan sang in 'All Along the Watchtower', 'So let us not talk falsely now / the hour is getting late.'

MATTIE MCG RATH

Politician

WHEN ONE looks at the scale of human suffering in the world, not only in the so called developing world, but here at home in the heart of Western Europe, it is easy to allow a sense of being overwhelmed to take over. As a public representative the sheer volume of need that crosses my path on a daily basis never ceases to amaze me. Without exaggeration, it is the privilege and the sorrow of the office. At times it feels like the work of Sisyphus rolling that huge boulder up the hill only for it to roll right back down as he nears the top.

I prefer, however, to concentrate on the practical aspects of what can actually be achieved and in that respect I take to heart the wise words of the 'Laughing Pope', John

First elected to the Dáil in 2007 for the South Tipperary constituency, Mattie MgGrath has established himself as a vociferous critic of austerity measures affecting the most vulnerable in society.

XXIII, who once said, 'Observe all things, change a few, and be silent about the rest.'

There is something very measured and hopeful in those words. They are a challenge to us and yet at the same time they remind us to be realistic about what can be done, if only to guard against a kind of fatal sadness that will undermine our ability to continue the necessary work. It remains true nonetheless that we can dream big and hope that even our own small efforts can have big consequences!

In light of the work of the Hope Foundation, that maxim is lived out by caring for one small and vulnerable child at a time. It is often said of deeply charismatic people that when they talk to you, you feel as if you are the only person that exists, such is their ability to connect in a meaningful way. I think that the work of the volunteers and staff of the Hope Foundation must be like that. I am sure the children feel that way.

Give me silent action over chatty but ineffective speech-making any day of the week.

They take one child at a time and work to draw out of that child a sense of its own God given dignity. So I suppose change in the world begins and ends in the hearts of the people who seek to do such things, despite the heart-breaking pain of encountering a starving child.

Words are fine things. They can win you all sorts of accolades and 'success'. But it is what we do when the speaking stops that really matters. As the Good Lord says, 'It is not those who say "Lord, Lord" who will enter the Kingdom of Heaven, but those who DO the will of my Father.'

Give me silent action over chatty but ineffective speech making any day of the week. We live in a culture that endlessly proclaims from the rooftops the 'rights' of people to live in dignity and yet at the same time crushes the poor and the marginalised. It is a contradiction that has become settled as 'just the way things are'. That is not an attitude I subscribe too. Change is possible. Hope is possible. We will never have a utopia but we can certainly diminish on a vast scale the level of suffering experienced in our world; even if we have to do it one child at a time. It is far better to do that than the lazy alternative of resigning ourselves to inactivity. As Helen Keller once put it, 'kindness is a language the deaf can hear and the blind can see'. So be kind and change the world one child at a time.

PETER MCVERRY

Priest and campaigner

SOME TIME ago, I was asked to present certificates to students who had spent some weeks working in very poor communities both in Ireland and abroad. They had to report on their experience to the rest of the school. I was particularly struck by one group of students who had gone out to Africa and worked with children who were very physically disabled and at the same time lived in extreme poverty. They reported that these were the happiest kids they had ever met: they had nothing, and wanted nothing. And they contrasted them with their own peers who had everything and wanted more.

There are two simple words that have caused untold suffering, despair and even

The Peter McVerry trust was established in 1983 by Jesuit priest Peter McVerry to tackle homelessness, drug misuse and social disadvantage. Since then it has supported thousands of young people on the margins of Irish society.

death to millions of people. They are the words 'I want.' Those two words have started wars and been responsible for countless murders, rapes, robberies: *I want Crimea, I want an Islamic State, I want your property, I want your girlfriend, I want your life.* Ireland has been brought to its knees by a small number of men – all men! – who said, 'I want more money.'

But these two words have not only caused immense suffering to others, but they bring deep unhappiness to the people who speak these words. For their unhappiness lies in the chasm that exists between what they want and what they have. The failure to bridge that chasm leaves a dissatisfaction which prevents peace both within the person, and between that person and others. It creates a constant restlessness which can never be put to sleep. Even if they finally obtain what they want, they quickly desire something else and the restlessness re-awakes, often even more virulently.

To build a world in which we can all live in peace and equality, it is necessary to replace 'I want' with 'you want.'

Unfortunately, the economic system within which we live promotes this restlessness and dissatisfaction. It encourages us to want what we do not now have so that we will go out and purchase it. The more we spend, the higher is economic growth. Without this consumer spending, economic growth stagnates or declines. But as our basic needs remain more or less the same, millions of euro are spent on advertising designed to make us want what we do not need.

To build a world in which we can all live in peace and equality, it is necessary to replace 'I want' with 'you want'. 'I want' divides me from others as I seek to secure, often from others, what I do not have; 'you want' binds us together as I seek to secure what another wants. Solidarity replaces individualism. My concern for what I want, and my efforts to secure it, is replaced by my concern for what you want and my efforts to secure that. But the only time when people unite in solidarity is perhaps when they are at war, or threatened by war. Our world needs a new war, a war on poverty.

There are so many unmet, basic needs in the world: one billion people living in destitution, millions homeless, living on the streets of every city in the world, millions more who are refugees from their own country, millions without clean water or access to cheap but lifesaving medicines, millions denied health care or education through poverty. The list goes on and on.

Meanwhile, I go on wanting the bigger HD television, the new car, the latest smart phone.

I dream of a world in which we all live together as a family. In a family, the parents do not give three of their children a steak for dinner and give the fourth child bread and jam. No, in a family, whatever we have we share. In a family, the parents do not tuck three of their children up in a nice war bed and tell the fourth child to sleep outside the front door on the porch. No, in a family, what few rooms we have we share. In a family, everyone looks out for everyone else, everyone cares and shares what they have, everyone carries each other's burdens. I dream of a world in which all people love each other, care for each other, share with each other, respect each other. I dream of a world where no-one would be hungry and have nothing to eat, where no-one would be thirsty and have nothing to drink, where no-one would be naked and have nothing to wear, where no-one would be sick and have no-one to visit them, where no-one would be in prison and rejected by their community.

Now, as then, there are many who do not want this dream to become reality. There are those who accumulate the world's wealth to themselves, while one billion people live in destitution. There are those who abuse their power for their own self-serving interests while people wait in poverty and powerlessness for the changes which could transform their lives but which those in power resist. There are those who will not reach out to the homeless, the drug user, the prisoner, those in social housing, but will reject them, want nothing to do with them and push them to the margins of their society.

Global economic growth, on its own, cannot build such a world. Such a world can only be build by love, by replacing 'I want' by 'you need'.

ROISIN MEANEY
Novelist

JANE ALWAYS looked like she'd got dressed with one eye on the clock, or possibly in the dark. The few items of clothing she possessed had seen better days, and their uncertain fit suggested that Jane might not have been their original owner. Her carelessly combed greying hair, unflattering glasses and teeth that looked like she'd never sat in a dentist's chair did nothing to dispel the notion that here was a woman who gave little or no thought to her appearance. In addition, her bony frame hinted at a level of undernourishment. As my mother would say: 'You'd give her tuppence'.

Over the course of the year that our lives intersected, I never gave Jane tuppence. She never looked for it. When we met, which was

In 2001 Rosin Meaney entered a 'write a bestseller' competition and won a two-book publishing deal. Since then she has had nine adult novels and two children's books published, and she has made the Irish top five fiction list three times. Her latest book is *The Reunion*.

every weekday at two o'clock, I was greeted with a smile and asked how I was. Jane's dishevelled appearance notwithstanding, she never once hinted that she might need help, and consequently I never offered any.

Jane turned up each afternoon to collect Zoe, one of my junior infants. She brought her home and looked after her until Zoe's mother, a single parent, had finished work. This was as much as I was told about the situation. Now and again I did wonder, seeing Zoe's smartly dressed mother when she dropped her daughter into school each morning, how the two women, so unlike in every way that I could see, had ever come into contact, and how the child-minding arrangement had come about, but Zoe herself seemed happy with the situation, and with twenty-six other little charges to worry about, it didn't concern me unduly.

Imagine everyone passing on the kindness they receive to someone else...Imagine the world we'd have then.

At the end of the year Zoe moved on with her classmates to senior infants, and apart from an occasional wave across the school yard in the afternoons, I had no more contact with Jane. The following year I spotted Zoe's mother coming to take her home each day, and assumed that Jane's duties in that department, for whatever reason, had come to an end.

It was to be several more years before we came face to face again. It happened on the street in the middle of the afternoon, about a week before Easter. By this time I'd given up teaching to become a full-time writer, and had had three or four books published. It felt like an eternity since we'd met, but Jane didn't seem to have aged a day. Not that I had ever been able to put an accurate age on her, with her unkempt appearance and general air of neglect. Somewhere between 40 and 60 would have been as close as I could guess, and she looked precisely the same now, nearly a decade later.

The clothes hadn't improved, or the teeth. The frame was as sparse as ever. I'd swear she wore the same pair of battered brown shoes that I remembered. The only difference I could see was the hair, by now completely grey, and the frown on her face. She told me her money hadn't come through and she needed to buy food, and would I be able to give her a loan?

I guessed the money was some kind of social welfare payment. I opened my wallet, intending to give her a fiver – and discovered that the only note I had was a fifty. A lot more than I'd intended to part with, but I could afford it. I handed it over, and she threw her arms around me and promised to pay it back. I doubted that I would see it again – she didn't look for any future meeting, or means of contact – but it didn't bother me.

For the rest of the day I felt wonderful. I went to bed feeling wonderful. The next morning I got up feeling wonderful. I walked to my local library to tell stories to tots, like I did every Saturday morning, and when my session was over the librarian handed me a fifty euro book token as an Easter gift. The storytelling was a labour of love; the only payment I got was a gift every now and again, usually book-related.

There is a street musician I often come across in town who plays the most beautiful music on his violin. When you toss a coin into his instrument's case he rewards you with the sweetest smile. He's from somewhere in Eastern Europe, and I sense that his command of English isn't all that good. One year, a week before Christmas, I baked a batch of cookies and brought them into town. When I found him I presented them to him along with my usual few bob, and he thanked me with the same lovely smile. When I got home from town I checked my e-mails and there was one from my agent telling me that Italy wanted two of my books.

I'm not sure what any of this means. I do know that carrying out any act of kindness makes me feel as good if not better than the recipient – and I find that I generally experience the benefit of someone else's kindness not long afterwards. I like to think that some cosmic force is keeping an eye on us, and making sure that what goes around comes around.

Recently I came across the phenomenon of paying it forward, which is simply finding random ways to keep kindness in circulation by doing something nice for someone simply because someone else has been nice to you. I've heard of drivers pulling up at a road toll booth and paying not only for themselves but also for the stranger in the car behind – how lovely is that? And then there's the suspended coffee movement that cafés have begun adopting, where customers are offered the chance to pay for an extra coffee which will be poured when a person in need claims it – wonderful.

Imagine everyone paying it forward, passing on the kindness they receive to someone else in whatever way they can. Imagine the world we'd have then.

But I can only do what I can, and as far as I'm concerned, kindness rules. Kindness always makes a difference.

MICHAEL MURPHY

Farmer and businessman

HANNAH ARENDT was a Jew, born in Germany in 1906. Though often described as a philosopher, she rejected that label because 'Philosophy is concerned with Man in the singular', and her work as a political theorist centres on the fact that 'Men on the ground live on the earth and inhabit the world.' We all face tough choices where we have to examine our conscience and beliefs as to the right thing to do, and sometimes doing it can be a tough and lonely pathway.

She quickly understood the evil nature of Nazism; and was active in getting Jews out of Germany. Arrested in 1933, she managed to escape to France thanks to the decency of a German police officer. In 1940 she

Michael Murphy has farming interests in Ireland, the US, and New Zealand, and holds a number of directorships. He is very interested in helping younger people to strive for excellence.

was interned in Southern France, but escaped, this time to New York. Hannah had a distinguished academic career, and published several highly regarded books.

In 1961 when Alfred Eichmann was put on trial in Israel, she volunteered to cover the trial for the New York Times. Hannah strongly disagreed with the idea of a 'show trial' where he would effectively be accused of all the evils of Nazism, despite the fact that he never actually killed anyone. (His role was to organise the train transport to the death camps). Six Israeli psychiatrists found him 'normal' and neither psychotic, nor anti-Semitic. At the trial he displayed neither guilt nor hatred, claiming he was simply 'doing his job and obeying the law of the land'. Eichmann consoled himself with the thought that 'he was no longer master of his own deeds', and unable to change anything.

Arendt coined the phrase 'the banality of evil' to explain Eichmann. She considered whether evil is radical, or the thoughtless obeying of orders by ordinary people; without a critical evaluation of the consequences of their actions or inactions. She was horrified at his inability to think for himself; and his total ordinariness, and mediocrity, hence the 'banality' of evil. She suggests that this strongly discredits the idea that all Nazi criminals were manifestly psychopathic; and intrinsically different from normal people.

Hannah insisted that moral choice remains, even under totalitarianism; and that choices have political consequences even when the person choosing is politically powerless.

'Under conditions of terror, most people will comply; some people will not. One is tempted to recommend the story of Denmark as an example of the enormous power potential inherent in non-violent action; and in resistance to an opponent possessing vastly superior means of violence.'

It wasn't just that the Danes, unlike so many other conquered peoples, had refused to assist in implementing the 'Final Solution', but also that when the Reich started to do the job itself, its own personnel in Denmark were no longer able to 'overcome their human aversion with the appropriate ruthlessness, as their peers in more cooperative areas had'.

Hannah concluded on Eichmann, 'Despite all the efforts of the prosecution, everybody could see this man was not a "monster". But it was difficult indeed not to suspect that he was a clown.'

Arendt's coverage of the trial was hugely unpopular amongst Jewish people everywhere, who resented Eichmann and other Nazis being depicted as clowns; and not evil psychopaths. Her description of it as a 'show trial' was greatly resented. She was accused of 'coldness and failing to sympathise with the victims of the Holocaust'. Her questioning whether the cooperation of Jewish leaders in the ghettoes hugely helped the Germans, created enormous personal animosity towards her. Her book on the trial was considered 'suspect' and not translated into Hebrew.

Today Hannah Arendt is viewed as a woman whose intellectual rigour and honesty eventually prevailed, even through the huge emotions unleashed by the holocaust. Her courage and honesty gives hope to anyone who believes in making the 'hard choices' irrespective of consequences. Thankfully, we always have freedom of choice; even in the most adverse of circumstances.

Rest peacefully Hannah. Your courage is an inspiration.

Hannah Arendt's courage gives hope to anyone who believes in making the 'hard choices' irrespective of consequences.

ELLIE O'BYRNE

Journalist

IN MY lifetime, I will have seen the population of the planet double. When I was born in 1980, there were 4.3 billion people in the world. It is estimated that by 2026, this will have risen to 8 billion. Even the staunchest anti-environmentalists must be beginning to wonder just how far we can stretch the earth's resources; sure, we could pack in 20 billion on a diet of sea algae, insects and genetically modified vat chicken, but that would make life a bit of a drag, wouldn't it?

The reason I bring this up is that it occurs to me that there may never have been a more important time for all of us to sit down and have a really good think about what we need to change in the world and how to go about

Ellie O'Byrne is a freelance journalist and media maker based in Cork.

it. "Be the change you wish to see in the world," is a quote widely attributed to Gandhi. Unfortunately, the quote has been somewhat abridged over time, perhaps to make it fit better on bumper stickers and on inspirational posters that some Facebook users are so enamoured of, the kind that come with a heavily photoshopped image of a sunset in the background.

The quote is good, even when abbreviated; it suggests that we start with ourselves in any change we are trying to achieve. Gandhi's statement was actually 'If we could change ourselves, the tendencies in the world would also change. As a man changes his own nature, so does the attitude of the world change towards him ... We need not wait to see what others do,' a far more powerful and radical statement, undercurrents of the activism and determination that made Gandhi the iconic – if oversimplified – figure he remains today.

I am lucky to have had a serious cause to question my mortality in my late twenties, and it changed my outlook for ever.

The notion of change coming from within is an important one, isn't it? We all know the story of the six degrees of separation; the one about the man who gets on the bus grumpy and shouts at the driver, and the driver in turn annoys another customer, and so on, until six people later the original grumpy man gets his come-uppance? Well it's true. We are a mass made of individual entities, like the sea-sponge. We ebb and flow together. Ideas and moods and hormones and mass panics ripple our surface. Our human reality is a consensus that we all help to form.

I am lucky to have had a serious cause to question my mortality in my late twenties, and it changed my outlook for ever. A rapidly growing liver tumour left me writing a slap-dash will one night. I was a 27-year-old mother with two young kids, hurriedly scribbling my wishes for my children and sealing them in an envelope to be left on the bed-side table when I went into hospital the next morning. A week after the operation, I discovered that the tumour had been benign.

I'll never throw away the letters I wrote that night, because they are a reminder of the second most useful lesson of my life so far, after the birth of my children.

Every time we pass up an opportunity, or hold back words that we want to say, or miss a chance to have fun, we forget that we live with death's gaze on us. Western society is increasingly death-phobic: strangers wash the bodies of our deceased, and the dying are sedated for the peace of mind of their relatives. Live close to your death and you live in full life. If we were more able to examine the reality of death, we'd revel in risk and chance and humour and seize every opportunity for positive change that came our way.

With this realisation in mind, I left hospital five days early and, more grateful than I'd ever been before, I came up with a list of principles I would live by, inner changes that I hoped – and continue to hope – would in some small way add to a world I want my children to live in. I constantly fail to live by them. Tiredness or self-doubt or financial worries trickle in while having to cook breakfast, or wondering why the cat is making that weird noise again. But anyhow, here are some of them. I still like them.

We are our own highest authority

Recently there's been a spate of click-bait articles doing the rounds with titles like 'You're not entitled to your opinion.' These are widely shared on social media by the spouses of the people who post the inspirational quote posters. The general gist is that we should shut up and allow those in the know, people with a formal education in a certain field, to do our thinking for us.

Disruptive innovation so frequently comes from outsiders who have a different approach, a multidisciplinary mind-set that doesn't slavishly adhering to the mythology of a profession. We will inhabit a very impoverished world when we lay down our brains and accept the status quo as expounded by somebody with letters after their name.

Each of us has a body of knowledge (sometimes, admittedly, amoebic) that is of value to our collective human experience. The conversation never ends.

We all contain the truth about ourselves and have done since birth. There is no higher authority than ourselves, as long as we're being true to ourselves. Our autonomy and inherent right to join the human conversation is not to be dispensed with; it is our birth right. This, I believe, is what Gandhi meant by 'We need not wait to see what others do.'

Question everything

Do you know the greatest speech by another great over-simpli-fied icon, Martin Luther King? No, not the dream one; the one where he thunders, 'I can honestly say that I never intend to ad-just myself'? He's stating his intention to remain maladjusted to a maladjusted society. Look it up; it's on YouTube. It gives me goose bumps.

All around us, stupid human systems based on archaic feudal-istic hierarchies are causing untold human suffering to people no different to you or me. The 'have' and 'have-not' mentality is indifferently propped up and supported unconsciously by…us. While we look away or allow ourselves to become distracted by the smoke and mirrors of the entertainment and media industries, the cycles of injustice and suffering continue unabated. We all have a responsibility to question our convictions and those upon which our social constructs rely.

Like a small child, we must probe, and keep probing, until we see that the answer to the final 'But why' will inevitably be 'Just because'.

Live in your body

We are animals. Just as a vegan cat in an air-conditioned apart-
ment is bound to be an unhappy animal, so a human being who
doesn't at least pay lip service to their biological adaptations is
bound to suffer. We aren't brains in vats (just yet) but we often
behave as though we are. Humans have evolved over millions of
years to expend energy, to experience hunger and satiation in cycles, to take pleasure in physical contact, and to suffer occasional
jump-frights. If you deny yourself these experiences, you won't
function properly. It's that simple.

Express yourself

It's a survival strategy: Swear. Dance. Paint. Make music. When
you're cross, find a good way to let the person know. Just express
yourself. You need to.

You always have a choice

When you pretend that you don't, you abdicate responsibility for
your actions. This must be the rule that I break most often. It's
easy to do; I say that I don't have the money, or the time. But really, normally what I should be saying is, I don't want to. I choose
not to. Act, and face the consequences. Don't act, and face those
consequences too. Adult life is a blessing. Even when it's terrify-
ing.

Fear is the single-most crippling human trait. Challenge it

Of course many fears have a rational basis; no, you shouldn't an-
noy that snake or jump off that bridge. But when the protective
mechanisms that arise from fear start to shut down our ability to
have new experiences, we've allowed it to become our master.
Fear provokes hostility. In human relationships, we often think

we're learning from past experience – our fear of hurt and rejec-
tion- when in reality we are just allowing them to taint new opportunities.

We use fear as a basis for learning, and in a physical sense that's
very wise. When my son was one and still unsteady on his feet,
he grabbed a hot radiator to steady himself. I picked him up, and
comforted him, and told him, those things? No, no, no. Uh-oh.
His pain and fear taught him too efficiently: in the summer, when
the radiators were switched off, he'd still look at them with worry
and say, uh-oh. In other houses, he'd suss out where the radiators
were and give them a wide berth. Uh-oh.

There's a natural human tendency to allow this form of learning to extend into the spheres of the intellect and emotion, where
they are counter-productive and limiting. A human is not a radiator; an uh-oh from one person is not a predictor of an uh-oh
from another. Staying open and expecting good things from each
human we encounter may seem unwise, and it can certainly lead
to more uh-ohs. But it's also exhilarating, enriching and enormous fun.

Love is an exercise of personal power and courage.

Try to love everybody you encounter. This is where my kids roll
their eyes to heaven and snort and fall off the sofa, but love as
a practice, an active discipline, a choice of outlook, is of enormous benefit in our increasingly crowded world. When you look
at someone and love them, you try to understand them. You see
their ugliness and frailty and preposterous complexity. This doesn't
make you a pushover, and doesn't mean you have to tolerate human stupidity and cruelty. In fact, it better equips you for communicating because you will come from a starting point of understanding. If all else fails and you're finding it impossible to
love someone, imagine them as a baby, at the moment they were
born. Babies are the stripped-back essence of humanity, beings of

raw potential. And yet through society's norms and inequalities we are variously formed and moulded, nurtured, loved, denied, stunted and repressed. There's no better way to generate love and empathy than to imagine each person as they first were. It's amazing who you can love when you put your mind to it.

Laugh, because everything is ridiculous.

It really is, when you think about it. Absolutely ludicrous.

GRETT O'CONNOR
Television and radio journalist

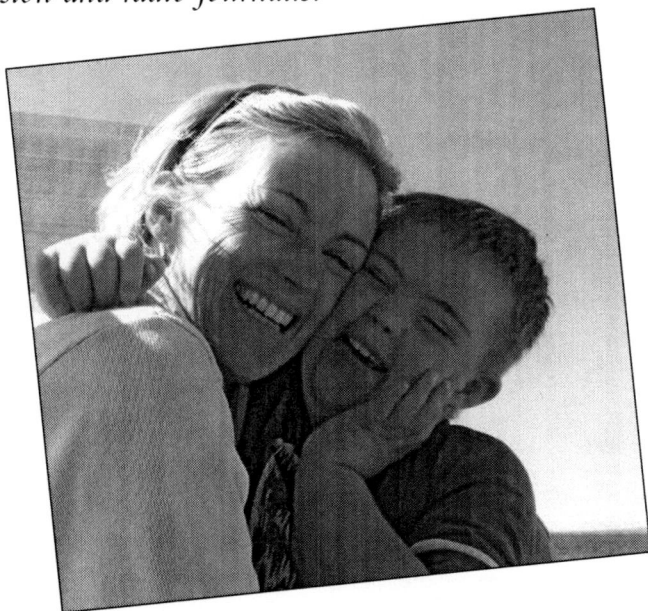

I DON'T have an exceptional voice but I love to sing. Of all the things I have experienced in my life, singing in the school choir back in the gloomy 1980s was among the best. It was so uplifting to hear all the other voices sing melody, harmony, a second harmony line – sopranos soaring, altos intoning, everyone part of the same well-oiled machine.

That's why I really wanted my children to experience the joy of singing in harmony. Three years ago I took on the job of coaching local school children to take part in a talent competition called 'Scór na bPáistí'. None of my own children were involved at the time, they were too young. I wanted to dip my toe in the water and see how it all worked.

Grett O'Connor is a TV journalist with Nuacht RTE and Nuacht TG4, based in RTE Cork. Grett presented the RTE Radio One political programme 'The Late Debate' in 2007 and 2008. Before her career in broadcasting, she worked for *The Kerryman* newspaper and also as a press officer with the Labour Party in Leinster House

Our local school is small and there are so few children in all the classes that putting a ballad group together is a bit like a lucky dip. Some years there are good singers in the senior classes, some years they are not so good. Either way, it is a great experience for them to learn two songs, including a little bit of my beloved harmony, and go up on stage to perform them in front of an audience of a few hundred people.

One weekend our 2014 ballad group (I share the coaching with another enthusiastic volunteer) took part in the county final of the competition – the final hurdle, as the competition doesn't go any further than that. One of my own daughters was a member of the group, also a nephew of mine, along with three other girls. They were runners up, they got their trophies and we all went home.

The enormous bonus of it all is the way my passion for these things brings about such a change in the lives of others…

But ever since I have been pondering endlessly the change this experience has brought about in my own child and in the others too. We practiced every single week for six months. We practiced twice a week before each competition. We practiced four times the week before the county final. In total, we saw those kids forty times.

We taught them to control their breathing. We taught them to listen to the notes of a song and reproduce them accurately. We taught them to tell a story when they sang. We taught them to look like they were enjoying it.

My own daughter learned to play the bodhrán because the ballad group needed one. She now says her bodhrán lesson is the highlight of her week. This newfound talent has made her grow in confidence. She has straightened her shoulders. She has lifted her chin. Another child in the group has undergone a similar transformation. Her performance in the county final was that of a girl who loved the limelight. Gone was the rabbit in the headlights we had seen so often before. She has blossomed.

You see, I have been trying to find answers to Gandhi's question for a few weeks now and I keep coming back to the ballad group. I love to sing, so I do it. I love to teach, so I do it. I love to hear people sing in harmony, so I make it happen. But the enormous bonus of it all is the way my passion for these things brings about such a change in the lives of others. It does a lot more for them than I ever set out to achieve.

It is too soon to say what difference these forty singing sessions will make in the lives of these children, and in the world in general. I can tell you now that they have made a big difference to me. I feel enriched and empowered by their success and their effort and their application. It makes me want to do more. Isn't that what 'being the change' is about?

FINBAR O'MAHONY
Management consultant

AS I walked down Patrick Street in Cork City back in the 1950s, smiling broadly as I went, a Capuchin priest approached me from the opposite direction. He was easily identifiable as belonging to that Order by the long brown habit tied with a white knotted cord that he wore, by the skull cap that covered his tonsure, by the wearing of a beard, his bare feet and open sandals, all signs that he was a follower of St Francis. As he drew closer he reached into the pouch at his chest and drew out a slip of paper and thrust it into my hand. The only words he said to me were: 'You have something very special there. Use it.' I smiled at him, thanked him, and moved on. The paper was the size of the holy pictures that popu-

Dr Finbar O'Mahony is a management consultant and has lectured for many years in strategic management, organizational development, HRM and psychology. He worked as a human resources director with a multi-national organisation and also as a programmer and systems analyst.

137

lated our Sunday Missals as page markers back then. I eventually looked at the paper and saw the words 'The Apostleship of the Smile'.

I think of that man frequently although I never met him again. I knew the members of the Holy Trinity Friary on Fr Mathew Quay but he must have been a visitor. Here was one man who had a simple idea based on his appreciation of the inordinate beneficial value of a smile. It is a universally recognised sign of friendship and is almost involuntarily reciprocated. It raises the spirits and dissipates negativity and anxiety. It is hard to simulate a smile without the falseness being easily detected. A genuine smile is like an emotional tranquilliser. It is a reassurance of a non-threatening interaction to follow first contact. I remember the Apostleship of the Smile: sharing the joy, sharing the hope, sharing the warmth of human kindness with those who have little or nothing of it in their lives at that moment.

What is the source of hope? What is the source of despair or desperation? What keeps us going when all seems lost? For me it is the example of two great women: my maternal grandmother Lizzie Hartnett and my mother Bridie who knew pain and loss in superabundance but survived. Grief is a natural reaction to loss and bereavement…having two or three children does not compensate for the loss of the third or fourth. 'But you still have us, Mam, and we love you' – the innocent words of a ten-year-old boy to the mother who had lost her five-month-old son to a knotting of the gut. Pain, real pain, cannot be soothed away by kind words. It has to be suffered until the bearer gets strong enough to carry on. To say that it will pass is to give false hope or show lack of understanding or experience. It does not 'go away', and it can be emotionally crippling but it can be worked through. If worked through for long enough it is possible to carry on.

Sickness, unemployment or poverty can either be endured grudgingly or borne with dignity. I would rather be rich and miserable than poor and miserable, but being miserable is a choice, so

I choose to remember the words of a late friend of mine: 'Happiness comes from wanting what you have rather than having what you want.'

Another chance meeting, one that happened years later on O'Connell Bridge in Dublin, also springs to mind. By now I was a married man with a little baby girl, a new house, mortgage, a job and studying for a postgraduate qualification. As I looked up I saw a small woman ahead of me on the footpath. She was collecting for her charity. She smiled at me as I had done at her as I approached. Her's was a beaming smile. She just said, 'Come work with me in India.' What an opening line! I explained my married state, my new responsibilities. She just shrugged her shoulders and spread her arms and then held my two hands and squeezed. I moved on. One of the younger members of her community stood further along the footpath and I asked her who the first nun was. She simply gave me the name by which she was known to her community. Yes, you have guessed the answer. She was the woman we came to know as Mother Teresa, now a saint. How different were the two situations, but how simple and direct were the approaches they made. Simplicity in the service of their belief and given with a smile. To see fear, despair, disappointment in the eyes of others is our cue to respond with support as that nun did, but in this busy world it is easier to hurry by to chase success.

Our experiences, even the toughest ones, can temper us like steel and give us the strength to carry on...

Now let's fast forward more than forty years to a spot on the road near the Village Green in Barnes in London. Again a smiling person approached and put out his hand in greeting, called me by first name, and asked me warmly how I had been keeping. I though this strange since I considered, mistakenly, that this was my daughter's next-door neighbour who lived not more than 300 yards from where we stood. As far as I was concerned, we had spoken the evening before. I felt that he had dodged a social visit that evening by telling me that he had to be in Berlin early the next morning for a conference. Yet, here he was. I asked him why he wasn't in Berlin. He looked puzzled. We parted and I nursed a little resentment at the imagined slight. It was only when I heard him being hailed loudly by a local outside the greengrocers about twenty yards away with a cheery 'Hello Chad! It is good to see you out and about' that I realised whom I had met but had not recognised: Chad Varah, founder of the Samaritans. We had known one another thirty years earlier over the course of two years or more and I had even bought him glass of dry sherry or two during that time. Here we had a man who knew the value of a smile, the reassurance of a firm handshake, the healing power of the warmth of friendship. He was a man who showed a zeal for service that not only changed people's lives but saved lives too. He had founded an organisation that spanned the globe but he kept his feet on the ground and did not lose his greatest asset, his capacity to empathise. That chance meeting reminded me of the crippling effects of resentment and the restorative power of hope and kindness. I learned valuable life lessons from Chad. Working with the lonely, suicidal or the depressed I learned about the genuine value of active listening – hearing what is said, what can't be said and what can only be said after much encouragement, building of trust, and an opportunity to untie the knot in the gut and untangle the barbed wire around the heart.

To some people the word hope can evoke a negative feeling. We have a choice to think of it in terms of 'more in hope than expectation', or in the words of the old song from my days in the South Mon choir, 'Whispering Hope', that went 'Hope for the sunshine tomorrow, after the winter has gone'. On the one hand hope suggests delayed gratification, satisfaction or relief while on the other hand we are bombarded with promises of instant gratification and exposed, at least by proxy or in a voyeuristic sense, to the luxury of the super rich.

A smile, a handshake, a hug might not save the world but they are a start in changing the world for someone. By such simple efforts are great changes wrought. Listening costs nothing other than one of the most precious resources we have: time. Active listening is hard work. The more we work at it the better we become and the more helpful we can be.

Many of us are familiar with the old debating topic: 'Events make the man, not man the events.' We are also told that there is merit in the African saying that 'it takes a village to raise a child'. The linking of those two ideas gives us a chance to see how everybody has a chance to change the world by their existence, and of course they are changed by it in turn. The circularity of the logic in the first statement begs the questions: which man? and which events? Our experience changes us, but we can use our experience to change others.

Our experiences, even the toughest ones, can temper us like steel and give us the strength to carry on regardless of the enormity of the obstacles facing us. Or if we choose, these experiences can become a corrosive force that has the power to destroy us from within. The power to influence others for good is a gift that is spread thinly in a world that sees ambition, worldly goods, status and achievement as the hallmarks of success. Real success is being available for those in need and it is best to start with those who are closest at hand. Kindness ripples out through society and in these days when we are faced with competing ideologies, opposing beliefs, and plagued by the loss of the social support of, and for, the extended family. If it takes a village to raise a child, we have long since destroyed village life in Ireland for all but a minority and we have suffered the consequences.

We never died a winter yet! 'Clonakilty, God help us' and the words of 'Skibbereen' are reminders of the defiance and pain that has sunk deep into the Irish psyche. Every part of Ireland has a historic litany of tragedies sufficient to depress the whole nation should we choose to dwell on them. Personal tragedy, ill health, unemployment, addiction can load us with an emotional burden that can cripple us, or they can be seen as the emotional furnace that tempers the steely resolve of the survivor. Our history has taught us about being the exile in the mind, but given some of us the strength to experience isolation without being lonely. It is easy to say 'What won't kill you will make you stronger.' How many times have we heard it when we least want to hear it?

The recognition and support of our community can change us forever. Such support can produce the finest people dedicated to the service of others and for the benefit of mankind. Some areas of my youth were described in colourful terms and some of the young lads were indeed tough. 'Poor, but dacent' was the expression frequently heard to describe some of the families. However, those same boys reduced the toughest priest I remember being in St Finbarr's South Parish to tears at Father Matthew Hall.

They accomplished that feat with the angelic sounds produced in the operetta *Zurika, the Gypsy Maid*. They had responded to the guidance of their choirmaster and teacher, Brother Dominic of the Presentation Brothers, and they also won the Thompson Cup in Feis Maitiú. By raising the aspirations and expectations of one cohort of students the community was changed; some students went on to second-level education, a few eventually went to third level and, at least one progressed to professional doctoral and post-doctoral studies. Is it too simplistic to say that all that change started with the setting up of a scholarship class, a choir and a school band? Hardly. The dedication of one or two men changed a generation and they in turn became the benchmark for following generations. The aspirational logjam had been cleared. So the events triggered by those men started a chain reaction that has been life-changing for many including myself. I ended up in the knowledge business and tried to pass on the same belief to others as was given to me.

Love works. Enthusiasm works. So do smiles, handshakes and hugs. I extracted a confession of love from my father two weeks before he died. As he lay there in his hospital bed I told him I loved him and he replied, 'Sure, I love you too, son.' From that I learned that I should never miss the opportunity to tell, and show, those I love that I do so. Showing is better than telling, so I have become a good hugger. Make it easy for others to love and be loved.

Not everybody is called to be like that good Capuchin with the handful of leaflets, not everyone can be a Mother Teresa and not everyone will be a Chad Varah helping the lonely, suicidal and despairing, but we can all help others, sometimes just by being there and, unfortunately, sometimes just by leaving. As I contemplate the challenges of the latter stage of life I realise that courtesy, kindness, justice, love, compassion and caring for others are the real changes that can be passed on as a glittering legacy. These qualities can produce the change in world that can easily lose its way in the headlong rush for material possessions and the search for the trappings of success.

A kind word costs nothing but is rarely if ever forgotten. It can turn a life around and set a person on a transformative road. We will be remembered not for how much we knew, what we were called, who we knew or how much we had in the bank, We will be remembered for how much we cared, how much we loved and how well we showed that love by deeds as well as words. As an old friend of mine was accustomed to say, 'There are no pockets in a shroud.'

So how can we be the change in the world that we would wish to be? Do as much good as you can with what you have, however little it is, for as long as you can, and for as many as are sent your way. We do not get everything in life right. Maybe we have to be content with getting some things right some of the time. That is not a bad start. We can change the world one person at a time by our actions and that person is ourself. Pass it on.

MATT PADWICK
Author

IT BEGINS with little things.

'What are you doing to prevent global warming?' The question – which was more like a wrathful challenge – was directed at His Holiness the Dalai Lama who had just finished consecrating a newly built temple in southern France.

The crowd went very still, now only His Holiness was smiling as he paused to consider an answer. So often we are presented with problems that are as big as the planet. How and where do we start?

'When I leave a room I switch the light off,' His Holiness replied.

It was said with such love and sincerity that the questioner was completely disarmed.

Matt Padwick was the manager of the Dzogchen Beara Meditation Retreat Centre on the Beara Peninsula in West Cork from 2003 to 2013 when he left in order to concentrate on writing. His first novel *Running Contra Diction* was published in 2015.

145

For me the answer was not about lights and saving electricity it was about personal responsibility. His Holiness was not excusing himself, saying he had other worries, or that it was none of his business and try to deflect the issue to the relevant authorities and experts.

I have many times marvelled at what a practical and profound response it was. It reminds me that taking responsibility and making a difference does not mean we have to be powerful or rich, and we do not have to become overwhelmed or stressed. It can be as simple as making a few healthy and pragmatic shifts. Imagine if we *all* switched lights off, and we *all* did not let the tap run while we brushed our teeth, and we *all* did not fly or drive when we could take a train or walk...

A positive attitude and a calm mind will not solve all our problems but it will bring the solution much closer.

Trends and fashions begin with inspired individuals.

Buddhist teachers sometimes borrow the environmental slogan 'think globally, act locally', saying we can apply it to our own lives, because they know that every action has consequences. While their view is all-embracing they would never underestimate the power inherent in one small action. They call it karma, we call it the law of cause and effect.

A keystone of their philosophy is that we live in a world that is by nature impermanent and interdependent. That means that every object and every situation is constantly changing, and dependent on numerous other factors and influences.

With this understanding it follows that even if we are able to make one, small, apparently insignificant change it *will* effect the whole. Maybe not dramatically, and possibly not immediately, but the next day we can bring another improvement. In this way we can be *in* the change rather than feeling like a victim of circumstances – we are more empowered and hopeful. Our perspective has shifted from what is *happening to us* to what *we can do about it.*

Sometimes just by knowing and believing that things are always changing, and that they will not always keep getting worse, is enough to help us lift our chin and face our difficulties. If I don't like what's happening sometimes I just remind myself to wait five minutes. Because in five minutes it will be different. If I let it.

In that light, stopping for five minutes, being physically still and allowing our mind to rest and come home to the present moment, is a very precious habit to cultivate – and a real investment in the future. During this time we are not becoming a captive audience for the voice of our favourite fears and concerns, we drop them too. As we quietly become aware of our breathing we will see that the voice is nothing but history and speculation anyway, and for these five minutes we are only interested in what is *now.* And particularly this fact that everything is always changing, we focus on that.

As our breath comes and goes we witness the truth of that.

A positive attitude and a calm mind will not solve all our problems but it will bring the solution much closer. We could use the analogy of when there is no wind and the surface of a lake is calm, and everything is clearly reflected. In the same way when our mind is calm we have more clarity and discernment.

Learning how to calm my mind has changed the way I look at people and circumstances, which in turn has changed what I see, and how I meet situations. Through Buddhist teachings my view has become more spacious and, I believe, more authentic. It is contrary to my modern, western education where I was encouraged to form a strong personal identity, measure myself against others and strive to best them with clever strategies, speed and aggression. The result of that mindset is alienation and anxiety.

For sure, some people have more fortunate lives than others but I have begun to see that no-one has only pleasure and no pain. And no person has the praise who will not one day receive the blame, or will always lose and never gain. And that ignominy is all that is left after fame. As I reflect on this, and how other people share my own aspirations, and my fears – how fundamentally other people are *just like me* – I am gradually liberated from the clutches of pride, jealousy and anger.

Each day, in small ways, I am changing.

One area of progress, which has also helped me bring about effective change in my world, is my gradually increasing readiness to accept things exactly as they are, now.

What? To effect change by accepting everything as it is, surely that is a contradiction?

Not really. Accepting *what is* is the perfect platform from which to assess, decide and deliver. Acceptance is balance and equipoise, and starting from that place the result is always better. If I compare it to my other 'settings' such as *chip on the shoulder* or *an axe to grind*, or *ants in my pants*, or *bull in a china shop* there is no comparison.

Accepting things calmly and clearly as they are is better by far because what fills my head determines my facial expressions, body language, and drives my actions and speech. But it not only inspires how I am, and what I say and what I do, but also how I *see* others – and how they perceive me. Quite significant then!

Hardly the private, secret world I sometimes think it is...

If my mind is the root of all I say and do, and everything has consequences, we would probably all agree that a positive intention or motivation at the beginning of any action or project is critical.

So what is the most skilful motivation?

Well, everyone wants happiness, and they want to avoid suffering. So we may like to make a heartfelt wish that our thoughts, words and deeds move us and others (who are just like us) in this direction – away from suffering, and towards a lasting happiness.

Often things do not turn out the way we hope or intended but from a Buddhist perspective if our intention was genuine and altruistic we cannot fail. So if an outcome is outside of my wishes and expectations I am comforted by the fact that I began with pure and positive intention, and I did my best. I remember that any outcome is the result of many interdependent circumstances – most of which are beyond my control.

I always try to be positive. If things are falling apart I look for, and focus on, what is working. The Zen master Thich Nhat Hanh says that the quality of our life depends on the seeds we water. He recommends we water the seeds of joy

In this spirit I begin again, more intelligently.

Finally two more from His Holiness.

'Never give up' and 'The truth will prevail.'

Coming from someone who must have had every reason to want to give up and to doubt the power of peace and goodness, they are powerful words indeed.

ALAN POWER
Head gardener and radio personality

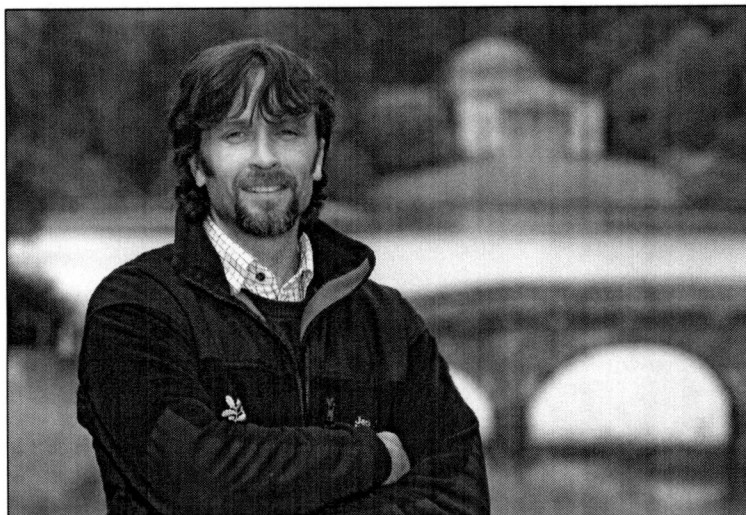

PEOPLE MEANDER their way through the network of roads that serve the English towns and villages that dot the countryside around Stourhead; they eventually find their way through the car park and on to the garden entrances.

Stourhead is one of the finest landscape gardens in Europe, and I would argue, in the world. Wrapped in and protected by the rolling hills of the ancient landscapes of Wiltshire, Somerset and Dorset, Stourhead has evolved over the past 300 years around a valley originally called 'Paradise'. Before this period the land was occupied by the Stourton family from 1448 until the early 18th Century. Human settlements have been recorded here

Alan Power grew up in Cork and studied horticulture in England where he is now head gardener at the historic Stourhead gardens in Wiltshire. He is a regular contributor to BBC Radio 4, captivating audiences with his wonderful descriptions of Stourhead at different times of the year.

since before the Iron Age. Lived in, admired, journeyed to, shared and recorded by millions of people during the centuries, Stourhead deserves the fame and importance it receives. Folk travelled across Europe and from America to admire Stourhead in the early days. Its fame and talk of its beauty spread fast and within fifteen years of its conception, before it was fully complete, it had gained national and international recognition from the experts at the time.

After almost twenty years working in and now managing the garden and estate at Stourhead my love and commitment to the place grows every day. Often referred to as a pleasure ground in the past, the garden at Stourhead has far exceeded the original ambition of the owner Henry Hoare in the early 18th Century. Not only is it a pleasure to gaze upon at all times of the year but it is also a wonder to explore and experience with close friends, family and loved ones. It's an experience to be shared, talked about, treasured and passed on. This is one part of the work I do that really moves me, when I witness the heartfelt way in which the beauty of Stourhead can take one over I am genuinely emotional. I feel proud of the work we do and achieve at Stourhead.

Conservation is said to be the careful management of change, it's about sharing and revealing the significance of places and ensuring their special qualities are enhanced, understood and protected for present and future generations. I feel that statement sums up my job description and it thrills me that I have ended up in a position in life where the work I do can really make a difference to the lives of others. Stourhead is one of the busiest gardens in the National Trust and we receive up to 400,000 visitors on the property every year. These people visit for many different reasons: some come to study the deep history of the place, some come for the wonderful collections in the house but others come through a sense of need and to escape from their day to day. Many have established a family tradition of visiting Stourhead that has existed for generations, and I meet others that are here as a result of a childhood memory and they want to recapture that moment before it's too late. People step further and further from their cars, they lose signal on their phones, lose sight of modernity in the landscape and then they have escaped for their moment; they are lost in the beauty of the place, silenced by the spectacle before them.

Even if it's just for that moment, I feel I have made a difference to their lives…and given them a little peace.

Sharing this wonderful place goes far beyond the physical and geographical property footprint for me. When I see the change in a person having seen and experienced this living work of art for the first or the twenty-first time I know its powerful impact must go further. I have taken Stourhead to the minds of radio listeners, TV watchers, newspaper readers and lecture theatres.

For me though it's the radio interviews that make the difference. I am lucky enough to be invited onto BBC Radio 4 to the PM program presented by Eddie Mair. The request is simply to describe what I see as I look at the garden during the autumnal display. I have done this now for six years and never realised the impact it would have on me or on some of the four million listeners. People have responded to me and said that they managed to escape from their place to another magical place for the few minutes as they listen. This escape for some can be from a traffic jam, a bus queue, a busy day in the office or a cranky boss. But for me the emotion builds as I become aware of those mentally escaping from hospital beds, from care homes, those less privileged and those also escaping from the real pain life has dealt to them. Even if it's just for that moment, I feel I have made a difference to their lives, maybe changed their path a little, described to them a picture of Stourhead to paint in their minds and given them a little peace.

SUZANNE POWER

Author, broadcaster and columnist

THE INITIAL equation: *Failure, plus rising above it, plus effort, equals achievement.*

I failed maths, but this equation I understand. You learn it all from your failures. They encourage change, they inform next steps. The best failures occur because you tried. To be change you must allow yourself to be changed, and the only way to change is to risk, and the risk is uncomfortable You feared it wasn't going to work but you had to give it a go. Flat on your face is still a softer option than not facing up to anything in or about your dreams.

Mortgages take twenty-five to thirty years on average to pay off. Regrets can last a lifetime if you decided not to take chances because of a mortgage, or a job, or a fear that

Suzanne Power is a successful novelist with worldwide sales. For many years she was a columnist for many of Ireland's newspapers and magazines. She has worked as a broadcaster, writer and reporter for BBC, ITV and RTE.

you would not meet someone else.

I've left possessions behind twice in my life to start again. The first time I took a rucksack and gave the contents of my flat on loan to a colleague to collect on my return from world travel. I never saw her or my stuff again. The only thing I missed was my guitar and I couldn't even play that properly. The next time was infinitely harder, leaving someone who I had shared over a decade with and married, with a car load of possessions this time and no home of my own to go to. Leaving all that love and history behind to find more of who I was. Like in *Tuesdays with Morrie*, I've always felt a nation should be within oneself. I think Morrie might have read Seneca: most powerful is he who has himself in his own power.

There are too many stories to keep telling the old ones. I am in favour of a life over a practice of regret.

I know that I've grown up a bit more when something I used to view as a failure no longer gives me hot flushes because I don't see it as one any longer. I love the line in the Kavanagh poem 'From Failure Up': 'Is the music playing behind the door of despair?' If you view life as a hero's journey, if you 'follow your bliss' as the great writer and mystic Joseph Campbell coined it, you have great moments, not always the ones you would have prescribed for yourself. In my late teens, through pure fluke I landed the big job in the big office in the big city with the big view from a big skyscraper. The truth was at 19 I just wanted a small life, in the countryside, in the quiet, with my big dreams inside me. I had never lived in a countryside or had a quiet life. But we all have a prophetic sense that's trying to inform us and it took the failures to get me here.

In the eighties that was a notion I couldn't yet afford and I was still contributing to the rhetoric, looking for success. I sat in a demilitarised zone between old-guard bon viveur journalists and new technology, slavish working hours advocates. I liked the bon viveurs, I beavered hard with the other side, Thatcher's children. I didn't join either camp. That was my story and still is. I left quietly, always. Back to the quiet. The career race was an illusion. The race is to the centre of the self. BMWs don't get you there. Walking is faster.

'Once you become familiar with the design of fate's illusions/ Your ink-well will contain all of life and death,' the Chinese poet Hsu Yun wrote. He lived to be 120 years old and was a monk for a century, living the last of his days in a cowshed despite having a reputation for venerability and a massive following.

My failures have taken care of fate's illusions. I have been sacked a good few times for what I now see as being honest. But then I felt stupid and sad about it. Today I believe everyone should be sacked at least once. If you're lucky enough to do what you love and marry who you love from the word go you maybe don't need to screw it up. But most of us don't get that lucky. Walking away from what's not good for you takes courage.

A woman over 90, Brid Murphy, who spent thirty-three years as a nun and lost her mother at 15, who was born as the Civil War bullets flew, told me after I had interviewed her, to enjoy my life. She is certainly enjoying hers. None of her crises prevented this. I think this is why the word 'emergence' is a letter away from emergency. She continued to love and gave me example in telling me this.

There are no medals, only love. The poet Rumi says: 'Love has taken away my practices.' Loving yourself through failure is vital in learning from it. Forgiving yourself and others are the shock paddles to restore deadened hearts and experience.

There are too many stories to keep telling the old ones. I am in favour of a life over a practice of regret.

The next equation is more complex, applied maths, failed that too. But I wrote this equation out of my life: Failure, plus rising above it, plus effort, plus reflection, multiplied by sincere forgiveness and love – equals achievement.

FRANCISCO REBOLLO
Author and airline pilot

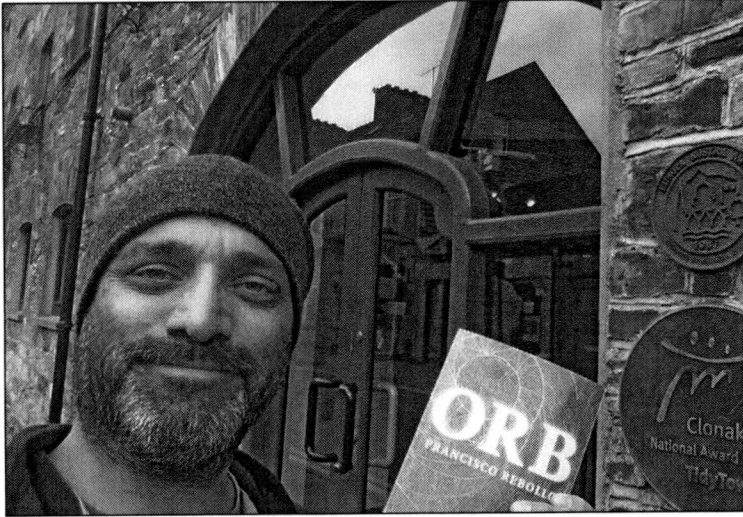

SOME YEARS before I was born, my father – an airline pilot – and a couple of his pilot friends went up to the Baja peninsula on a golfing holiday.

One day, for something different, they hired a local fisherman to bring them out fishing on his small vessel.

Baja is a mars-red desert peninsula in Mexico. The land is like a thousand different kinds of fire, the sea flows in a myriad of colours from jade to purple and everything in between. The water is transparent and the sand is powder-white.

My dad and his friends were Mexico City pilots and, as such, they were unusual: wealthy men who did a glamorous job, lucky men –

Francisco Rebollo, from Mexico, works as an airline pilot in Ireland and is a novelist and poet. His novel *Orb: An Aeronautical Love Story from an Altered World* was published last year.

159

or so they thought, and they had brought their big-city frame of mind on to that small boat with them.

My dad and his friends sat as passengers as the much poorer Baja fisherman piloted the boat out to where the good fish were. As they sat there waiting for the first bite, the fisherman asked them a few questions, speaking from under the straw hat that protected his already-obsidian face from the midday sun.

'Hey *Capi*...' he said to them, (*Capi* is a common abbreviation of *Capitán,* or Captain, in Spanish, as in airline captain.) 'Where do you guys fly? How fast does your aircraft fly? What kind of engines are on your aircraft?'

He got into the technical side quite a bit. You could see he was interested in aviation in general.

When he felt he was becoming a pest, he reverted to a platitude and asked about living in Mexico City - the densely populated, quite polluted and land-locked capital of Mexico – a world away, over a thousand kilometres in distance and over eight thousand feet above sea level.

After answering the fisherman's questions the men sat in silence, still waiting for the fish to bite. All looked around and someone remarked on the breath-taking beauty of the scarcely populated paradise that is Baja.

'Do you think I should buy a house out here?' one of the pilots asked the fisherman.

'Well, it depends on what you want out of life *Capi,*' the man answered.

Since the fisherman was younger than the pilots, one of them thought to take an interest in his own plans for life. 'Would *you* like to live in Mexico City someday? Maybe attend college sometime? UNAM in Mexico City is free. You could attend.'

The fisherman looked at the pilot who asked him that questions and asked in turn: 'Why would I want to do that?'

All the pilots looked at the man. Another replied: 'Well, you seem technically minded, you could go on to become an engineer, a pilot…or whatever you want, there are opportunities out there, waiting for you to snatch them!'

'And why would I want to do that?'

'Well, after you graduate and make some money from your chosen profession,' another one said, 'you could travel and buy a house somewhere amazing and go fishing there…fishing, but for fun!'

The fisherman looked around at the pilots. They got the sense that they were not really getting through, until he responded.

'*Capi,* I am already fishing for fun, and I already live somewhere amazing.'

Ever since I heard this story, the image of the 'fisherman in Baja' has become part of my personal mythology, my ideal of success: the contented man who will not waste a second chasing someone else's goals.

I often think of this story when I find myself making plans years ahead of time. Years ahead of right now. Thinking of places that are far away, places that I'd like to see but probably won't.

This story also taught me to throw away any prejudgments I might have in my head about other people. Everyone is wise, there is no one 'right path'. Many people are wealthy in ways that we can't see. If you can be can be happy right now, if you can see the beauty around you, wherever you are, then you already are a complete success in life.

I want to be like that fisherman. I want to value my place in the world and enjoy what I do for a living. The only opportunity I want to snatch is the opportunity to be content with my lot. To be thankful and enjoy what I'm doing.

It remains to be seen whether I'll ever be a fisherman in Baja.

GILLIAN RIORDAN

Psychotherapist

WHEN I finished college my first job was working as a social worker in a psychiatric hospital. As part of my work, I would take these detailed case histories at an out-patient clinic, which made me very aware of the different needs of the people attending the clinic. However, they were all put on the same five drugs no matter what their age, situation or need. There was no talking time.

This led me to seek out training in psychotherapy. I worked as a psychotherapist for over twenty-two years in Eckhart House in Dublin. At this point I took a break – I wanted more. Psychotherapy wasn't giving me all the answers. I found another training which focused very much on psychology and spirituality and

Gillian Riordan trained and worked as a psychotherapist for twenty-two years in Eckhart House in Dublin and then went on to study with the I Am University. Her main work now is facilitating learning and healing sessions in West Cork.

how they are both necessary to our growth and psychological health. This made such a great difference in my own life and my own understanding of myself and the causes of suffering.

I wanted to share this knowledge and help others to learn and heal.

I worked with people individually and ran some groups but there was more I needed to do. I had this vision, for a number of years, of setting up a Centre of Learning and Healing in West Cork – I deeply felt that we need to think in new ways about what we are experiencing personally and at the community and world level.

We are all so held in materiality as if the world we experience with our five physical sense is all there is. We have limited ourselves so much, got so disconnected from self and the within and from Nature. We have become so caught up in approaching our problems always in the same old way – over and over. And what do we get? More of the same. Our major concerns are with what we think other people think of us, the fear of not getting it right or of being wrong and the need to feel safe/okay. We are so busy fitting in and not listening to our own inner sense of things. We are so caught up in managing the outside world and our idea of success.

We live as if we are an ego, a personality and a physical body and so we feel constantly under threat. We have forgotten who we are and what life is all about. We believe in lack – lack of money, of jobs, of love, of opportunities – lack generally. We talk about it a lot. We believe in sickness too and talk about it a lot. There is great fear around.

I think the time has come to question all the old beliefs and attitudes we hold and to expand our understanding – try new ways. Why do we hold onto these old beliefs and attitudes and never question them? Why do we accept so easily all that we are told through the media and medicine? Why do we listen to the ads and allow them to programme us? Why do we get all upset about emotive news items and spend a lot of time giving out about these instead of getting involved to make a difference in our world? Why are we hell bent on finding someone to blame instead of taking responsibility and seeking out ways to help solve the problems in our world?

Each one of us can make a difference.

It's time to realise we are not just an ego, a personality, a physical body. We are Soul and we are connected to all people and to the earth – we are all interconnected.

We are all here to make a difference in whatever way each of us is called to this.

The understanding that the wisdom we need is within is something we may have heard about but it doesn't seem to be something we live. We have a belief that the answers we are looking for are out there, outside of ourselves. There is no time given to seek the answers within and no sense of trust in the answers and ideas that come from within.

I think the time has come to question all the old beliefs and attitudes we hold and to expand our understanding…

My vision is for a Centre of Learning and Healing – a place where people can question old beliefs and attitudes, understand what causes suffering and learn about what will not only heal, but, also renew and build spirit and life. It's a space where people can come together and share their questions; a space where people have the opportunity to gain psychological and spiritual insight and understanding, work together, share ideas and issues, have the support to live what they are learning, break out of old limiting beliefs and discover new solutions.

For almost two years now, I have been running group sessions for the purpose of providing this kind of space for people. Some have been coming weekly for a lot of that time. There are three different groups running here in West Cork and one in Dublin, so far.

These sessions are about having an opportunity to learn the kind of things we haven't learned at school or very much anywhere else as we were growing up. In more recent years many may have read or heard about these ideas but most likely haven't had much opportunity to explore and live them. There is such a difference between knowing something and living it – so that it makes a difference in one's life.

So much of life is lived on the surface. So much of conversation is surface stuff, disconnected from what's going on for us. People 'talk' about things. People rarely talk about what deeply matters to them – the uncertainties and questions they have about life. So much of the time we are living outside of self, disconnected from the Soul within. This is the cause of so much of our suffering. We need to make time for learning and growing at a psychological and Spiritual level so that we can really live, feel connected and find more meaning and purpose.

There is very much an attitude of doom and gloom in response to the economic changes and challenges of this time. People generally feel disempowered and there is a 'wait and see' attitude, a belief that change will only come from the top down, from the government, from sources other than the people generally.

We are resource rich and we will fully realise the extent of these resources when we come together, collaborate together and keep our focus on what we want and making this happen.

We have a choice to see opportunity to grow in new ways and create more and better or to see doom and gloom and things just steadily getting worse and harder. The choice is ours.

Our focus needs to be on what we want and not, on what we don't want. We listen too much to the media and think this is the truth. We listen to this and so fail to notice what **is** working and the opportunities that are there for us to grow into a much richer and deeper understanding of who we are and what life is all about.

We can create a culture of health, interconnectedness, sustainability, trust and prosperity for all.

The sessions we hold aim to provide a space for people to come together, think together, learn, build ideas and create solutions. Working together for the greater good of all and renewing our minds and Spirits are what will move us forward to make a difference.

When we cooperate and work together anything is possible. The solutions that come from people working together for the greater good are indeed powerful, great and effective – they frequently amaze.

Together we can do it. What are we waiting for?

DAVID ROSS
Farmer and pastor

MOST PEOPLE on the American continent consider the "Top of the Rock" to be the observation deck on the seventieth floor of the Rockefeller Center in New York city, built in 1933. Its magnificent views across New York have delighted visitors for the past eighty years. By contrast, Ireland's 'Top of the Rock' can boast a history reaching back to the venerable St Finbarr of the sixth century. He came here because this was already an ancient meeting place where people gathered around its two standing stones of antiquity. St Finbarr is known to have preached the gospel on this spot. A stone church was built nearby, the hallowed imprint of which may still be seen today. My life story began in this very place

David Ross is a farmer and pastor of an evangelical community based in Bantry, Co Cork. He is founder of the Drimoleague Walkways network and proprietor of Top of the Rock Pod Pairc, a unique family farm accommodation and walking centre in Drimoleague.

in 1959. It was here that I played in the fields, built stacks of hay in the hayshed and learned the stories of the people who lived in Drimoleague before me.

On New Year's Eve in 1978 I found myself standing on my own at the midnight hour at the Top of the Rock. I was 18 years old and my life stretched out before me. The frozen moonlight air served to sharpen the outline of the Castledonovan hills and the cheerful lights of some thirty scattered homesteads flickered in the distance. After all, it was still Christmas in Drimoleague. Suddenly I became aware of the presence of God, so that for one hour all I could to do was to worship and sing and pray to God with a joy and a peace that was unlike anything I had ever experienced before. It was like Heaven invading this heart of mine. That night I asked God how my life could make a difference for Him, and I clearly remember my face turning in a westerly direction to Bantry and beyond. I knew instinctively that I was called to bear the light of Christ and carry the very thing that had changed me …the good news of Jesus.

Mahatma Gandhi knew the need for inward change. The words 'How can I be the change that will make a difference in the world?' are said to be a paraphrase of a fuller version: 'If we could change ourselves, the tendencies in the world would also change…' Gandhi knew that our primary need was that we should change our own nature. The question is, 'Can this be done? Can we lift ourselves up by our own bootstraps?' The Christian message, which Gandhi held in high esteem, declares that the God who created us is the only one who can truly re-create also. The change must come from above and echo deeply within us. In Christian terms this involves repentance, faith and the following of the One who gave his life for us on the Cross. It was this message that changed me as a young teenager and gave me the confidence that God was changing me each day and would bring change in the world around me too, as I walked closely with him.

In 1982 I married Mary. There was a beauty and simplicity about her faith in God that attracted me to her. We believed that together we could make a difference. As we built bridges into Bantry's diverse communities, we found all sorts of creative ways to share the love of Jesus. Our kids' camps, prayer groups and home visits brought people together on one great quest. Those who looked to Jesus for salvation, peace and mercy found what they were looking for.

At that time we did not appreciate that change could occur through suffering, but when Mary was diagnosed with breast cancer while carrying our third child, we came to see that God will also use the crucible of suffering to change our hearts and those around us. Her death brought forth incredible amounts of sympathy, kindness and compassion. Paradoxically, Mary's full confidence in Christ pointed many people to the reality of heaven and how Jesus has made a way for us to be there.

Coping with loss and bringing up three children on my own was a tough but rewarding assignment. I learned that providing a secure foundation for my children was more valuable than anything I could do in community or church. They had only one dad and I needed to fulfil that role which nobody else could fulfil for them. Nearly four years later I married Elizabeth. I am grateful for her selfless dedication to myself and the children and to their two siblings who were born subsequently.

Church is something we have taken for granted in Ireland for centuries, but when you feel a calling to bring together a new church you have to do some serious thinking about the nature of what a church community is, where it originated and how it will be sustained. For me the local church is a most powerful agent of change because it is built with very fallible people and yet powered by an infinitely almighty God. For twenty-two years Elizabeth and I have been on the leadership team of an evangelical church in the heart of Bantry. Here up to eighty people meet every Sunday. They comprise every age group, many nationalities and a wide variety of temperaments, opinions and expressions. They are drawn together in a common life around the Cross, where all our sins, failures and disappointments are met with the undeserved grace of God. We therefore meet on level ground around the cross of Jesus where God is at work changing lives every day. Church is not the product of one person doing all the work. Church is every member being empowered to go back to their home, workplace and community every week to live out the change Jesus has brought about in them. In this way change multiplies quietly and perceptibly.

I am a work in progress, but the God who created me continues to change me every day.

Change is also about our part in the community and landscape where we live. This is where I am drawn back to the Top of the Rock. For thirty two years I have farmed this parcel of land which runs down to the Ilen river. I know its thirteen fields like I know the back of my hand. It was passed on to us and we merely serve as the custodians of it while we are here. My time has seen remarkable changes in Irish agriculture, yet I am grateful for the encouragement given through the REPS scheme and other initiatives to draw out the full environmental potential of this farm. Trees have been planted, habitats preserved, fertile ground planted with bird cover, old species reinstated, and stone walls preserved. The cumulative result is pleasing to the eye.

In 2007 I gave leadership to a small group of farmers in Drimoleague who set out to bring the Sheep's Head way eastwards to this parish. As a result, some 12km of walkways were created in the beautiful landscapes surrounding the Ilen river and Mullaghmesha mountain. We aim to present the heritage of Drimoleague in written, audio and walkable format to increasing numbers of people, who now find themselves drawn to these hills and valleys for recreation, exercise and reflection. Seventeen farmers have kindly opened their lands under the Walks Scheme. The older generation have been involved in passing on their heritage to the young who have embraced the work of preserving and presenting it. Business in the village has increased as people arrive for a few days walking. They need provisions, taxis and accommodation. Drimoleague has risen to the challenge and has certainly seen change for the better.

The Top of the Rock has once again assumed its ancient role of being a meeting place. Until 1988 I was unaware of the tradition of St Finbarr's pilgrimage from this place. Then one day I was contacted by Denny O'Leary from Skibbereen who said he planned to ride a horse from Skibbereen to Gougane Barra by way of a pilgrim journey, a tradition which his parent's had passed down to him. Would I send him on his way from the Top of the Rock with a prayer? That simple request and the prayer that Denis and I made to God that day prompted a fresh understanding of my calling to be an agent of change. I rediscovered the oral tradition of St Finbarr in Drimoleague which states 'in the sixth century he admonished the people to return to Christ, and then he went on his way to Gougane Barra'. I also discovered that groups of pilgrims used to converge here from all over West Cork to walk to Gougane Barra.

By 2009 the pilgrim path from Kealkil to Gougane was already reinstated by an active community group led by Dan O'Sullivan, and in a remarkable convergence of four local community groups in Drimoleague, Mealagh, Kealkil and Gougane the St Finbarr's Pilgrim Way (Slí Bharra) was re-opened. Today this 37km pilgrim path takes its place among the sixteen leading pilgrim paths of Ireland. Each Easter and twice in August, groups of up to seventy people take the two-day reflective walk. Many others walk it in small groups throughout the year, particularly on September 25, the feast of St Finbarr.

Because our home has always had an open door, it seemed natural to extend this welcome to the increasing numbers of people who were turning up at the Top of the Rock. After a great deal of

prayer and consultation we submitted plans in 2012 for the Top of
the Rock Pod Páirc and Walking Centre. Two years later in June
2014 Eamon Ó Cuív TD opened our accommodation and walking activity centre. Situated in what remains of our grandfather
Sam Ross's stone-built farmyard, we have seven timber lodges
known as camping pods. The walking centre contains the bath-
rooms, kitchens and a large meeting area which can accommo-
date up to seventy people. Families, couples and walking groups
converge here from all over Ireland and beyond. The Top of the
Rock is once again a meeting place of joy, activity, laughter and
reflection.

By way of conclusion I quote the 'The Serenity Prayer' au-
thored by the American theologian Reinhold Niebuhr (1892–
1971). The best-known form is:

God, grant me the serenity to accept the things I cannot change,
The courage to change the things I can,
And the wisdom to know the difference.

There are things that still need changing in my own heart and
in the world around me; I am a work in progress, but the God
who created me continues to change me every day. I know that
one day I will be with my Saviour Christ, who once laid down
His life for my sins. I cherish my freedom to live in the joy of His
forgiveness, acceptance and amazing grace. It's all a gift…and it
can be yours too for the asking!

PETER THOMPSON
Journalist

LET US now praise famous men, and women, indeed, and let us also take a good hard look at them. In my view, it's a good starting point for considering the question of how you go about Making Change, given the perils of attempting to do so.

In an 'age of uncertainty,' to use the late JK Galbraith's famous phrase, how do you change things for the better? This is challenging, when we seem to be living through a time when, to use Rudyard Kipling's (also) famous words about keeping your nerve, 'all about you are losing theirs and blaming it on you.'?

Speaking of Kipling – and indeed of Galbraith, who was US ambassador there –

Peter Thompson is a native Dubliner. He was educated there at Trinity College. Having worked as a grain merchant and a teacher, unsuccessfully, he then became a journalist ('As you do,' he says). He is a long-time contributor to *The Irish Times* and was formerly also a theatre critic with *The Irish Press*. He now lives in south Wicklow.

brings me to where I wish to start this discussion, and to two of the three people, one, a man, the other a woman, I shall consider in making my initial contribution to it: India. It is perhaps symptomatic of our present age that we start far from Ireland, and outside Europe, and, by coincidence, in the very country where the Hope Foundation does its work, the vast sub-continent where so much of the future will now unfold.

Mahatma Gandhi and the recently-canonised Mother Teresa were, undoubtedly, people who were the change. Gandhi was of course the man who gave us the challenge to 'Be the Change,' instead of waiting around for others to be it instead. Mother Teresa, I think I can reliably inform my readers, was someone who really did effect, and for the better, such change.

In changing for ever the lives of countless thousands of the poorest of the poor in Kolkata, one of the most socially challenging places on Earth, Teresa was 'The Change.' She also challenged, by her personal lifestyle, some of the cherished myths which today, not just in the West, but it seems everywhere, that one should strive only, for oneself, for a comfortable, materialistic life with plenty of financial security, scanning the latest jewellery or yachting catalogue to purchase the next ever-more expensive object with which to enhance our lives.

Mother Teresa achieved what she did this against great odds, but at least the Indian state was not actively against her project, so far as I know at least.

Gandhi, however, when he commenced his journey to Indian, and by extension all human liberty, did so against and in the teeth of opposition from, the British Empire, at the time the world's only superpower. It proved to be a long and extremely difficult journey. The obstacles included not simply the overwhelming military superiority of his opponents, but, arguably, the greater obstacle of the *mindset* of his opponents: a deeply ingrained, and as we now know utterly deluded, sense of racial superiority. It was a mindset which led the British down cul-de-sacs for decades in the last century and not only in India!

It was Gandhi's great achievement to have liberated India without the use, or endorsement, of violence. His message of passive resistance and the use only of democratic methods has resonated down the decades. It was to inspire the US Civil Rights campaign of the 1950s and 60s, and of course the Civil Rights campaign in Northern Ireland at the end of the latter decade. Martin Luther King's example very probably owed much to Gandhi, as the northern civil activists' did to King.

But let us stand back, for a moment, from all this fine worthiness of people who were 'the Change,' and consider a third person, like Mother Teresa, a woman, who was also 'the Change.' Her name was Margaret Thatcher, and with her mention we enter a more complicated territory of 'being the Change.'

Uncomfortable as it is for those, like myself, on the social democratic left politically, in the 1970s Britain was held to ransom, too easily and too often, by large trade unions who were, in effect, unaccountable. Their leadership was elected by a fraction of their membership. It was often intractable and blindly opportunistic. Something had to change, and in 1979 it did, when Mrs Thatcher came to power after the infamous 'winter of discontent.'

We now know, in my opinion, that much of what followed was frankly disastrous: there was too much economic change, too quickly, with communities in the industrial parts of Britain – and Northern Ireland – decimated socially in an ill-advised rush to turn a great industrial nation into a 'services economy,' a term which is perhaps an oxymoron.

But what cannot be denied was that Margaret Thatcher was the Change, that she provided outstanding, steely leadership, particularly during the Falklands crisis. She was also an extremely able politician, in controlling her party and parliament for eleven years as Prime Minister. Inevitably her luck ran out when, to adapt another famous phrase, of Denis Healey's, she was savaged by a dead sheep called Geoffrey Howe, whose bitter resignation speech in the House of Commons was the beginning of the rusting of the 'Iron Lady.'

What, I hear my readers ask, has all this to do with a hope and heroism? Everything, as it happens.

With the present, 2016, US Presidential election in mind as I write, we have reached a crucial turning point in Western society where the creators of our contemporary heroes, the mass media, are concerned. Let us return to our three game-changers for inspiration here.

In his time, Gandhi was very largely misunderstood by the majority of the British media, and equally misrepresented by large sections of the Indian one. He also held views which might well be seen as backward today, such as his De Valera–like vision of India as an autarky of self-sufficient villages. His practice of bringing girls, some prepubescent, to bed with him, in order to test his commitment to chastity, at the very least would raise eyebrows today.

Mother Teresa, during her lifetime, was very strongly attacked by writers such as the late Christopher Hitchens, among many others, for holding views which also appeared backward, even to the point of pointless anachronism. These included her apparently blind obedience to an increasingly reactionary Vatican, and her opposition to family planning and to abortion in all circumstances.

Today, Margaret Thatcher's infamous remark that 'there is no such thing as society,' albeit often taken out of the context in which it was spoken, is a symbol of the crucial fault-line in her thinking. When the financial markets collapsed in 2008, it quickly became apparent that in a fundamental sense, to quote Fintan O'Toole, 'there is no such thing as private enterprise.'

In other words, people who are, 'the Change' are not perfect. They are flawed, we all are. They get things wrong; we all do, sometimes for a higher motive. Churchill and Roosevelt had to ally with Stalin, a dreadful mass murderer, to defeat Hitler.

With Gandhi, Mother Teresa and Margaret Thatcher in mind, and indeed Donald Trump and Hillary Clinton, propaganda, not nuance, is the name of the game for the vast majority of the output of media which appears to need hero-worship. Our modern Homers and Virgils, on TV, radio, in films and in print, are the makers of our modern heroes. They, regrettably, also make our modern demons when perhaps they should be more discriminating there, also.

And so to my pitch, my attempt to Be the Change. Let me fly a very big kite here, not, of course, that anyone will notice, their attention distracted elsewhere by those very mass media, the Bread and Circuses of the contemporary world.

If, as a species, we are to survive, then an essential part of our survival strategy must be a global media law…

It's this: in the future we need media which are totally owned, in every aspect of their operations, by charitable trusts, removed from all State or private interests. Such trusts would be obliged to inform the public of what it is essential that it be aware. These issues include climate change; the reality (as opposed to the wishful thinking of electoral-cycle politics) of economics; the obligations of international law including human rights law; full truthfulness about food including its sourcing and preparation; and the full and open disclosure of everyone's source and amount of income, wherever it is stashed.

Utopianism, I hear readers howl. Well, let me put it this way. If you had lived in, say, 1890, at the age of 20, and had been told that, if you lived to be 80, you would be able to have breakfast in London and dinner – albeit at a late hour - in New York on the same day, you might well have answered 'that's utopianism.' If you had lived in 1950, aged 20, and you had been told that, if you survived until 80, you would be able to instantly communicate, with total clarity as to both language and vision with somebody on the other side of the world, you might well have replied 'that's uto-pian.'

Of course, both of my examples relate to developments in technology, not politics and law, and therefore, in the words of Kant, may not apply to 'the crooked timber of humanity from which nothing straight was ever made.'

But consider this: who anywhere, in 1950, aged 20, would have believed it possible that, by the time they had survived to be 85, men would be able to marry men, and women, women *in Ireland*, of all places!?

If you had been a young soldier, aged 20, in the Allied or Axis armies, in 1942, would you have believed, recent developments notwithstanding, that by the time you reached 80, you would be living in a world where global war would be unthinkable, as, in fact, it is, despite ongoing tensions between the West, Russia and China? Would you have replied 'that's utopianism'? You very probably would.

My argument is that if, as a species, we are to survive, then an essential part of our survival strategy must be a global media law, rigorously enforced, which ditches propaganda, and replaces it with fact, and honest opinion. This does not mean that all dissent would be banished. Far from it, but it would have to be honest-ly-expressed dissent. Essential herewith would be a change in the way we do discussion publicly, so that it is calmly expressed and presented.

It is important to stress here that a trend in technology globally may assist us here. Developments in neuroscience are today lead-ing to a greatly enhanced understanding of how our brains func-tion, including such functioning under stress. Apply such knowl-edge to debate, and you change the nature of debate itself, to see more clearly what the reality of issues are, to see, for example, that something is what it *is*, and it is not something else.

Such a law, such a practice, might well put an end, for example, to the Nazi-type rallies we witnessed in the current US Presidential election. It might also put an end to the (to me, at any rate) ridiculously self-serving confrontations which pass for virtually all political and parliamentary debate at least in Ireland, the UK and the US. It would get rid of spin, incidentally a term derived from cricket to describe when a bowler is *deliberately trying to deceive* the opposing batsman or woman.

But first, we must have hope, that word the use of which helped to transform Barack Obama's first Presidential campaign in 2008. To quote the words of the man who was, in my view, his greatest predecessor, Franklin Delano Roosevelt, we need to remind ourselves that 'the only thing we have to fear is fear itself.' With the collapse of certainties which accompanied the outbreak of global war in 1914, hope seemed to have disappeared. Now, as we venture further into the 21st century, we need to remind ourselves that a clear-eyed hope is an essential part of our future.

JOHN WATERS
Author and journalist

EVERYONE IS unique. That's more than an axiomatic platitude – it's also a reminder of something our cultures seek to deny in the name of what is called reason or progress.

Each of us is a subjectivity – an 'I' – that has never existed before we arrived and will not recur after we are gone. This is our value, what we offer the world. Our world tries to suppress this in the name of 'objectivity', or 'rationalism' or scientific empiricism – forces which more and more bear down upon the human person, telling him or her that there is no value in the subjective, that truth is possible only by entering into a 'detached" and 'neutral' view of reality.

Whenever I speak to aspirant journalists, I

John Waters is the author of nine books as well as being a sometime playwright and song writer. He writes regularly for the *Sunday Independent* and *Irish Independent*, and was a columnist with *The Irish Times* from 1991 until 2014.

emphasis this. I say that I cannot teach them how to be journalists or writers – I can only awaken in each of them the awareness that what they can offer the world is something no on else can: in each case the totally unique subjective position before reality that no one else can replicate. I tell them to listen to as many other people as they can, soak up the experiences of others, enter into the witness of other people's lives – and after that make all of this their own, processed through their own experience and perspective. That's what's of interest: the unique testimony of a single witness.

…we must all accept our individual burdens of responsibility to speak out against the increasingly distilled mentality of the mob…

Too much of what we think of as opinion in this apparently highly-opinionated world is merely received prejudice or propaganda – regurgitated by voice after voice for fear of seeming different, or out-of-step, or politically incorrect.

If we had been around fifty or sixty years ago, before the advent of mass media society, we might have fondly imagined that the evolution of mass communications such as television, internet, 24-hour news and wall-to-wall commentary on every tic and twitch in the public and (increasingly) private realm would have enabled every human person to have a voice to speak of what is real and true and enduring and beautiful about being human. In fact, the opposite has happened: these technologies have served to drive back into the throat and heart of everyone the impulse to speak of truth and beauty, and instead subjected each of us to a minute-to-minute pummelling of ideological prescriptions, the demands of lobbyists, economistic cliché, manipulation, bullying, intimidation and every form of obscenity thrown down by way of challenge to anyone who would still insist on the right of the human person to speak of human dignity, hope, love or grace.

In the face of these growing obscenities, we must all accept our individual burdens of responsibility to speak out against the increasingly distilled mentality of the mob, and speak instead of the human heart and its longing for great things. One of the great challenges facing us is the development of a language to express an authentic sense of outrage about the abuses of truth and meaning perpetrated by innumerable ideological interests so as to silence all dissent about their various assaults on human dignity. Against this, there is only the 'I' – the unique subjectivity out of which each of us can state the only knowingness that is possible in the world.

9 780993 114335